A RELUCTANT LIFE

A WIFE'S JOURNEY THROUGH LOVE AND LOSS

To Relly —
I hope you will
cry a little but
enjoy it as well —
Yvette

YVETTE NACHMIAS-BAEU

CHESHIRE HOUSE BOOKS
NEW YORK

Design & Photographs: Yvette Nachmias-Baeu.
Other photos: George Guiterrez, Bengt Karlsson, William Morgan, Frank Hellgardt
Bio Photo by Seth Jacobson Studios, RI.
Production: Bernard Chase

Website: www. AReluctantLife.com

ISBN 978-09675073-09

LIBRARY OF CONGRESS CONTROL NUMBER
2011934119

To Dieter
Bonds are made from the best part of who we are

Acknowledgments and Gratitude

Many people stayed in the room with me, witnessing parts of this journey. I am particularly grateful to my son Jesse, and his father Dean Saglio, Seth Jacobson, Kate Vivian and Ellen Hellgardt, for the way they let me know how much they cared. To Nicole and Malcolm Spaulding, Ulana Farmer, a physician, a friend, and a comforting presence. To Ann and Dennis Gannon, who witnessed the beginning, the middle and were there at the very end, still holding my hand. To Joyce and Jerry Fingerhut, Ron and Laurie Millican, and Mary Ann Scott. So many more loving friends, who saw my husband and me through this extraordinary time. One begins to understand the magnificence of friends and family.

There are others, who took the writing of this book seriously, encouraged me and gave me their precious time, their wisdom and talent, to move this project along. Gratitude is not enough, but when I can replace it with something more, I hope to be able to bestow that on you as well.

A special nod to Eileen Landay, a talented writer, a lover of language, and a generous friend who advised me on portions of this book. To Mary Gae George, an inspiration, and one who knows first-hand what grief means. Thomas James, Dee Ito and Mark Hammond, it is my sincere pleasure to be your friend. And to Anthony Alicata—who encouraged me and held my hand, I give you my abiding friendship and love.

Stuart Ward, for generously editing this manuscript, giving me license but never a long leash and pushing me to dig deeper. His knowledge and love of literature informed the work and kept me true to myself.

Linda Stewart, who proved to be as a lioness devoted to a cub, as she continued to fine tune this book. Her store of knowledge is simply breathtaking.

The question that most concerned you, Dieter, was not really simple. You spent your whole life wondering about what life was for. You started asking yourself that question when you were a young boy, and since there would never be a simple answer, you reluctantly decided to let life reveal itself. You once told me that if you were ever to write a book about yourself, the title would be "A Reluctant Life."

A RELUCTANT LIFE

Dieter is now in his last descent. I don't know if he will survive the weekend, but I believe it is now days. He is declining rapidly. I think you must now be in Sweden, so I send this letter in hopes you will receive it in time. He is like a little bird quietly lying in his nest. Each breath becomes harder. He is not in a coma, but his body is beginning to shut down. I sit with him hour after hour, and tend to him as I can. The tears are endless. Dieter is leaving us, so please hope as I do, that he continues to leave as peacefully as he has lived these past weeks.

I have come to know him in a different way these past months. I am struck by what an honest and uncomplicated soul he has. He has never felt sorry for himself, nor has he ever shown any fear. He has accepted his illness with kindness and a generosity of spirit. It makes me realize what I already knew—that he always meant what he said—that he was always true to himself and to me; there has never been any subterfuge or guile. Those who know him, as you yourselves can attest, have found him to be genuinely unique, amusing, and profoundly confident. He did not suffer fools gladly, but has always been kind to those who were genuine and honest. He could spot frauds within minutes. He didn't condemn them—but neither did he feel compelled to give them his time. He accepted his own frailties, and tried to rise above them. So he leaves us now without a troubled mind. Those strangers who have taken care of him in the last weeks have been struck by his gallantry and peacefulness. I have no words to explain what I am feeling right now. A dark shade has been drawn around me and I am in considerable pain. But I do send this with love. I know you love him too.

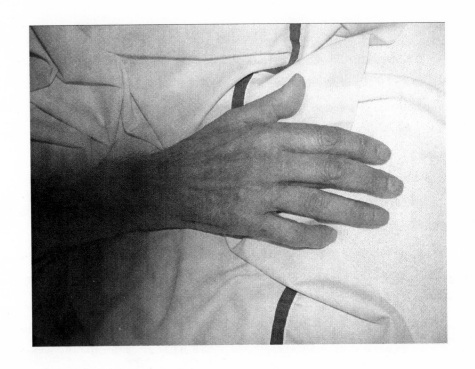

Dieter is gone! These are the words I hear as I enter the house. A short sentence—a simple fact. You are gone. Where did you go? I see that you are lying there half turned as you had been earlier in the evening. But now there is no breath. No life. I wash you down and cover you. I remove all the trappings and devices you no longer need. You are still warm. You lie there silently. I brew a pot of tea. Your color is changing. What is there to do? I have no thoughts. I sip the tea that is now getting cold. There is a sense of emptiness that may be what misery feels like. Should I play Beethoven's 9th at decibels loud enough to drown out my sorrow? I am without impulse. I feel that my life is over, except for the gestures and the strange need not to break down. I realize I can do nothing because there is, at this moment, nothing left to do. You are no longer here. I stand by your bedside, tears in my eyes blurring the image that will remain with me for all time, unable to believe that while you are here before me, you are no more. You are placed on a stiff board. The sound, as they zip up the black bag they have put you in, startles me. The descent from your house is made feet first as you are carried down the stairs for the first and the last time. The stairs that you built, that you used to climb daily and often. I find myself wondering if you ever imagined that this would be your final exit.

Who am I? Where have I been? What have I done? How is my past reflected in the view I have now? And why am I compelled to write about it? All I know is that I must. This is a time of loss for me. A death has occurred. I am witnessing my life through a different lens. So this becomes a time for review and reflection.

We often see things without focus, as though in a dream, and we devote precious time to wandering through our lives, not always really looking, or perhaps, unable to see the spiraling, multi-dimensional view of it. We look side to side, backwards and forwards in a linear progression, hoping that we might solve the mystery.

Perhaps the single most important thing for many of us, and the questions we often find ourselves thinking about, but are often afraid to ask are: Who am I? Can life be beautiful? How do I feel—and why? Then the real imperative is the overarching question frequently asked and often avoided—what is life for? Yet we continue to walk through life, because we have to, marching in place, or taking a few bold steps forward, reproducing, wondering if our experiences define who we are. We wonder if our relationship to others will help to clarify our place in the universe. What we do, what we say, whom we meet, whom we choose to love, all have value in our lives. Because we are in this life for only a short time, the blink of an eye, the questions resonate and circle around us continuously, while the answers come reluctantly and infrequently.

Matthew Arnold wrote in "Dover Beach":

Ah Love, let us be true
to one another! For the world which seems
to lie before us like a land of dreams
So various, so beautiful, so new,
Hath really neither joy, nor love, nor light,
Nor certitude, nor peace, nor help for pain;
And we are here as on a darkling plain
Swept with confused alarms of struggle and flight,
Where ignorant armies clash by night.

The experiences that brought me to the present moment—my life's walkabout—took me to remarkable places. My conclusions, if any can be made, suggest that the life I have lived so far has been the product that I created, or that I allowed to be created. So it brings me back to the first question. Who am I? In the context of my loss, I begin to see so many phases of my life. I fully understand the way in which life is episodic, and the images that confront me appear much like a crowded subway car at rush hour, all bobbing heads and limbs, looking for some place to fit. Memories begin to surface and come at me in fits and starts, decades overlapping one another, so that each memory vies for its own space. It is like a tapestry, bold, vivid, and complicated. This retrospective shows me the variable and dissonant tracks my life has followed. The parade of people who passed within my sphere gives me a sense of the extraordinary, sometimes fleeting connections my life has allowed me to make. The flow of that panorama of people in motion represents the space on earth that I have occupied, and I have found it baffling at times, largely because I have rarely, if ever, been aware of how I fit in.

14

I wonder, not infrequently, why there were so many people in my past who have gone on to become celebrated—whose attachment to purpose allowed them to achieve what most of us only dream of. For whatever reason, my life was joined to many people who would later become famous or successful—or already were. My own journey took me to far different places that were less visible and at times I felt, as Arnold writes, that we are here as on a darkling plain.

Does it define me that one of my first year-long love affairs was with Dustin Hoffman? Is it interesting that one of my girlfriends became Ann Getty, the wife of J. Paul Getty's son? Does it warrant comment that Robert Duvall spent a great deal of time in my living room, or that Shel Silverstein took me to dinner? That I danced on Anna Halperin's dance deck, was an original member of the San Francisco Mime Troupe, or that Dean Stockwell and I roamed Greenwich Village one September evening long ago? Will it change anything if I were to be remembered by well known people who once pursued me? In the larger scheme of things, probably not much.

What defines the early period of my life for me was the unfolding, and the recognition that it was my own life to live. I took on life with the exploratory exuberance of youth, and by doing so continued to move further away from the original trajectory most parents want for their children—the default position which many of us seek or adopt: a profession, a marriage and a family. That might lead me towards contentment, but as Wallace Stevens noted in his poem *Sunday Morning*, "in contentment, I still feel the need for some imperishable bliss."

By exploring this new path, I took myself to places that helped me gather the courage to live my life outside of convention, and to continue to move farther away from the life that had been laid out for me. I found I was living in the style I designed for myself or fell into it quite by chance.

I spent ten years in the theater, devoting that time to the pursuit of art, believing it might help me explore the questions on my mind and help make sense of what I wanted to believe could be found—a platform linking discovery and renewal to other people's lives. Though my first foray into marriage did not last, the product of that union was a son. In my new role as a mother, I experienced a genuine sense of beauty and wonder that came with nurturing and observing my child grow into the person he would eventually become. I started a school, became an entrepreneur. I was attracted by the spiritual nature of life. I learned to tend the earth, to garden, to milk a goat, to ride a horse through fields at speeds that took my breath away, and somewhere along the way I discovered that life is limitless. I learned to cope with and rise above the shattering experience of a deadly illness and was able to find my way to the other side. I wandered through the "groves of academe" for eleven years. Everything I touched or became part of, became part of me as well.

> *I am a part of all that I have met;*
> *Yet all experience is an arch wherethrough*
> *Gleams that untravelled world, whose margin fades*
> *For ever and forever when I move.*
> *Ulysses,   Alfred Lord Tennyson*

Now those years are gone. And for eighteen of those years, I did find in marriage the ultimate joy of being in total communion with another person and able to understand love as the true gift that life can, and occasionally does, offer. The decade I am walking through right now, the one that may well be my last, is the one in which I experienced a major passage—the most visceral, heartbreaking, and critical event of my life. It is this part of my story that I wish, need, to write about—to speak to those of you who have found, or will find, yourselves in this same place. The only difference will be in what complicated way you find to adjust and cope with what this extreme moment is about: the process of loss and grief that death brings into our lives. As I begin writing whatever this turns out to be— these widow's scratchings have taken on the form of an open and continuous letter to my late husband—I know it is a journey that even by the last page will not have ended.

I recognize that I am everywoman, no more or less important than that. Yet, I feel a strong need to share the daily experience that took over my life. It is exactly three years now that I have been writing these letters. I started during the onset of my husband's illness, and continued through the duration and complexities of that experience. I have continued to write in the solitude of my grieving, months after he took his final breath—letters that allowed me to continue the conversation with him and to chronicle what for me has been so profound and final.

I received a letter today from our friends who have shared so much of our life together. It arrived just days after your death. I am feeling dazed and torpid. You are not here to read it with me but it occurred to me that you might like it if I read it to you:

'Thank you so very much for the deeply moving words about Dieter. We have read it over and over again. We cry and remember events lived and felt together. I especially like to dwell upon our trip to New York and the unforgettable opera performance at the Metropolitan. That was our last meeting before Dieter got ill. And the tremendously fun Christmas we had at yours and Dieter's houses. I think it was the first time we met you! And then this thing and that comes to our minds. For Bengt, the store of memories after 40 years of friendship is without end. Dieter's life changed when he met you. We think it was the best thing that could have happened to him. He loved, and admired and depended upon you so completely, it is almost impossible to think that he could have had an existence before you. When we think of him, living alone, bereaved of you—it is not to be imagined. I think you are stronger, and however cruelly hard it is, and is going to be for you, we both have faith in your capacity to survive. You, together with Dieter, are almost constantly in our thoughts. Looking at his pictures—he is so beautiful, so incredibly beautiful."

The question she asks is one I do wonder about. Do I have the strength to survive alone? It all remains to be known. At this moment it is not clear to me. I will find out if I have the capacity to live without you, and hope that our friend's faith supports my ability to live a life worth having.

YOU WERE, YOU HAVE BEEN, YOU ARE NO MORE.

Our story is not unique. People die all the time. Each of us will by turns. We have that in common. So how is it, knowing this is true, I feel that I am unique? I am standing outside a door. The entrance is blocked and I cannot find a way to enter. At the door I hear whispers of all those suffering the universal pain of loss. I have joined the chorus with the dirge of lamentations and keening, yet now I hear my voice, more prominent, rising above all the rest as I ascend into a place that is mine alone. I find myself curiously detached, invisibly marked as a person alone, and I feel that I am the only one grieving. I know that the people you have known cannot grieve for you in the same way—a few perhaps. They have gone about the business of their lives. Of course they must. You know that I am trying to conduct my life as if I had one, but I am in limbo right now, and unable to say out loud what is always on my mind: You were! You have been! You are no more!

As I look back now, I am so much more aware of how things end. Once there was a time I did not think very much about endings. I was at the threshold of a beginning. What a powerful feeling, when your love is returned! There is an expansiveness of nature, a sense that you have arrived at a place that is brilliant and charming, the only place that you want to be. You are amazed that life can feel so beautiful, and overwhelmed by a sense of belonging. Everything is clear. It is an exquisite time and you wonder if it can last. And yet thoughts of endings are not on the horizon. There is the sense that this state of mind is permanent and that we will have all the time we need to be together and do something of value. And as I look back at the most mundane times of our alliance, the simple exercise of following through on necessary tasks—the grind of working, preparing meals, or general housekeeping— I always felt there was the promise that we would do something grand. Even in the least dramatic times, there was the sense that we would have another day and seek another challenge. And then we were given a challenge.

Now there are shadows in the hallway, your footsteps silenced, though I sometimes still hear them. This phantom sound stops me right where I stand, and I find myself asking out loud: Why does the end of life have to be so damn sad? Why do we live our life as though it were endless, and then are either snuffed out in a surprising second, or linger, altered to a point where we no longer know who we are, and, die in that alteration? The design seems flawed. What is the lesson? What are we supposed to learn? Then again, why do I think everything that happens is meant to have purpose and meaning? Are we obliged to pass through hard times in order to find some kind of sanctuary that could not be otherwise attained? How does our personal experience benefit the rest of mankind? Is it even supposed to? How is your death going to supply me with answers or direction? Is life supposed to have meaning?

Or is death a simple lesson in ecology? Perhaps we just live for a while, become useful for a time, ponder all the unanswerable questions, and finally, with no firm conclusions but with acceptance, turn our body in, so that it can be sourced out as parts for those still living, and hope that what remains will become part of the earth once again. Is there more than this? Does what we discover ever become the braided rope of wisdom that allows our souls to climb towards the truth?

THE DAY OUR WORLD CHANGED

You had been upstairs moments before to get someone's car keys so that you could move her car out of the way to allow the delivery truck to roll into place. You were preparing to deliver a large piece of furniture you had just finished. I had noticed that you stared at the keys in your hand for some time, which I thought odd but nothing ominous registered. How could it? We were still young. We had plans and the expectation of having many more years to live. How could I know that your hesitation heralded what was to come.

When I came to your office and saw you fidgeting with some papers that had little meaning to you, I became alarmed. I remember asking, are you okay? When you did not answer, it was clear something was terribly wrong. You began to speak slowly as if you were no longer inhabiting your body—'Yvette, my lovely wife." You could say no more. I called an ambulance. That is when you had your first seizure, and precisely at that moment, our lives changed irrevocably. Yours was now shortened to eighteen months. When the diagnosis came—Astrocytoma: brain tumor—you merely said that the news was disappointing. I said nothing

24

because I could not. I just bent my head and began to cry. Something heavy on my chest was stopping me from breathing. I began to shiver. My stomach was in convulsions. I couldn't wrap my head around the notion that after all these years of your remarkably good health impervious to anything resembling illness—you would become the victim of a disease that had no cure.

You were in my life for eighteen years and it hardly seemed enough. What would I do without you? How could I live without you? How could the day turn into night, the seasons change? How could there ever be Sunday again? Would I be strong enough to see you through this terrible time? When would I lose you?

This is personal. It is the beginning of a love story. We were just two small lives in a sea of lives, all with their own story, most of which are probably more interesting than ours. But everybody enjoys a good love story, and ours was a remarkably happy one, almost from the very start. I find myself thinking about the day we first met. I like to remember it, because now memories are important and precious, though also painful. How odd that so many parts of life seem invisible except when we recall them with our mind's eye, and try to find the words that might actually capture them.

> *in after years,*
> *When these wild ecstasies shall be matured*
> *Into a sober pleasure; when thy mind*
> *Shall be a mansion for all lovely forms,*
> *Thy memory be as a dwelling-place*
> *For all sweet sounds and harmonies;*
> *William Wordsworth, Tintern Abbey*

The moment I set eyes on you, I had a sense that you were the person that I wanted to spend my life with. I still can remember what you were wearing—though that is only significant because I can recall it. I can still see you as you were on that summer afternoon, taller than most everyone present. I noticed everything about you: your lean body, long limbs, blue eyes, and a voice, the sound of which I had never heard before. It was like marbles rolling around in a deep tunnel. And then there was your mysterious foreign accent and your remarkable diction. I could not place where you had come from. You were imposing and handsome.

I was in the midst of a new beginning, having just closed a business that I had operated for twelve years. I knew my life was changing but wasn't sure what direction it would take. I had no compass. I was like a forest creature, scratching to find some berries.

I noted you weren't happy to be at this backyard party, loud and full of children's energy, people, and volleyball. I could see this wasn't your idea of fun, but you stayed for a polite amount of time. You even participated in the volleyball game with determination, if not enthusiasm, and I was fully aware that I had not managed to capture your interest.

I do from time to time act impulsively. And this was one of those times, as if some spirit whispered in my ear that it was time to take a chance. It was time to know if there was anything at all in my attraction. Two days later, with hesitating fingers, I dialed your telephone number that had been left on the pad by my phone by a friend who had called you the day of the party. There was that distinctive voice again. I took a deep breath, and much too quickly explained who I was—hoping you would remember. When you said you did, I recall feeling relieved, and then blurting out, "I have two tickets to the tennis matches at the Newport Hall of Fame. Would you like to go?" You sounded astonished as you asked if I had known that you were an avid tennis player. I did not. You agreed to come with me. And so it began. I remember the wild ride in your butterscotch-colored BMW, gasping as you prepared to pass a car on a two lane road. I could see you were steady at the wheel, if heavy on the foot. I looked over at you as you drove, and realized how beautiful the lines of your face were. The particular fold around the cheek that accentuated the line that flows between the nostril and surrounding the corners of the mouth was a feature I found extremely appealing. And your legs seemed to go on forever. I could comfortably steal glances at you under the guise of conversation and I was not unhappy. You parked the car and took my hand to guide me down the street towards the Hall of Fame. The whole day felt warm—really pleasant and thoroughly peaceful. Neither of us made an effort to impress. We actually watched the tennis matches, perhaps three of them, before we decided to get a drink on the big lawn at The Castle on the Hill overlooking the bay—where, for the first time in that long day, we began to reveal little bits about ourselves. You took me to dinner. We walked hand in hand down to the waterside, and later you shook my hand goodnight at my door, thanking me for a lovely day, and suggesting I call again if I had any more good ideas! I suddenly felt I was in a Jane Austin novel. I wished that I had a calling card to slip into your hand. I felt let down. But I shrugged it off, deciding it was not important. The ball (so to speak) was now in your court. I had made a gesture and you would have to follow through because I wasn't aggressive enough to try this again. And then quite by chance, as I was having lunch on Thayer Street days later, I picked up a newspaper and began to read about the Tennis Hall of Fame. The writer said all the things we had said to each other, about what a beautiful place it is; how the grass courts and the close proximity of the players, were surely the best and most civilized way to watch a tennis match. I cut the article out and sent it to you. Two days later, you called to say you had two tickets to Saturday's matches and would I like to go. At the end of that day there was a kiss.

THE STAIN

Not long ago, I finally watched a film that you and I had wanted to see together. It became available after you had died, so I watched it by myself. Another story of the madness of World War II—a film you could have watched, because this was a small but powerful story about two people whose lives had been altered by the circumstances of war. There were so many films you could not watch because they brought you back to the horror of that war and the questions of your heritage.

All your life you carried with you guilt about having been born German. Clearly you felt an indictment had been placed upon your country, and you took the blame for the genocide. You were very young when the war was raging, and you had no part in its misery, yet the question of how these vicious acts were possible, was a question that would never leave you.

I remember the day we decided that we should see the movie *Schindler's List*. As a Jew, I also had difficulty watching documentary footage of this war and the hideous slaughter of millions of people. I had seen quite a number of these accounts, and the horror was mesmerizing, visceral and terrible. It still seems unimaginable that a madman was able to coerce an entire nation into his nightmarish visions. The misery and fear of the experience brought upon a people was impossible to watch. But we felt duty bound, in our late 20th century world, far removed from the killing fields of history, to see it. We didn't quite understand what that duty was. Perhaps it was that we were survivors, and therefore, should bear witness. We both realized at the same time that we could not watch this movie, no matter how brilliant or uplifting the story was. It was, after all, a very small victory in the larger scope of this tragedy. Without a word, we stood up and left the theater.

Within the context of this history, I recall another incident. It was still early in our relationship, but we were already connected. I was going through a stack of your photographs, an attempt at organizing them, when I came upon a picture of your father in his soldier's uniform. I stared at it for some time and found myself in tears. You looked at me with some hesitation and came over and hugged me, and gently said, "I knew this would be difficult." Then you tried to explain that your father had been a professional soldier, which was different from the SS or Nazi Party's army. I recently decided to understand more about the war and your father's place in it. This was something I hadn't fully investigated, and thought it was now time to learn more.

A LITTLE BACKGROUND

You told me you were born in the Black Forest, which always brought to mind an image of a baby in a white cradle, a shaft of sunlight falling on the spot where you lay, and giant fir trees hovering, encircling and protecting you. When you were still a toddler, your family moved to Silesia, an area marked by historical upheaval. What makes Silesia interesting is that it lies mainly in southwestern Poland. When you moved there with your family, parts of the region were then German, a token given to Germany as the result of the First World War. During World War II, Polish Silesia was occupied by Germany and became another site of atrocities against the population—first by the Nazis and later the Soviet forces. In 1945 the Allied powers assigned virtually all of Silesia back to Poland. But by then you were long gone, having moved to the Hessian region of Germany which was now occupied by the United States.

Part of what made our alliance somewhat symbolic was that we were born during World War II. We were both children of the war, you a German and I, a Sephardic Jew born in Bulgaria. What I know of your early life is only what you have told me. You often had trouble remembering personal things, or movies you had just seen a week ago, and books you'd recently read. But you never forgot what was truly important to you. You would for all your life, be conscious of the fact that you were born German. You wondered what you would have done had you been older and more aware of the political insanity and genocide of the day. You couldn't be entirely sure whether you would have succumbed to the fear of losing your own life had you objected. Not being absolutely sure made you cry at the sheer horror of what you later understood had happened. You held the guilt of your nation close, though you had been a very young child. Yours was later called the silent generation; the children who watched their families and their nation succumb to evil.

I remember that you stopped what you were doing so that you could explain the complicated structure of the German Armed Forces during the war. Your father, you said, was a professional soldier in the *Wehrmacht*, meaning "defense force"—the name of the unified armed forces of Germany from 1935 to 1945. Hoping to improve my understanding of the language as well as the structure of the armed forces, you carefully pronounced each word, saying that the *Wehrmacht* consisted of the *Heer* (army), the *Kriegsmarine* (navy) and the *Luftwaffe* (airforce). What was essential that I understand, was the difference between the *Wehrmacht* and the *Waffen-SS*, the combat arm of the SS (the Nazi Party's paramilitary organization). You conceded that the *Waffen (SS)* did become the de facto fourth branch of the *Wehrmacht*, as it expanded from three regiments to 38 divisions by 1945. But the SS was still autonomous and existed in parallel to the *Wehrmacht*. You felt it was important to make that distinction.

Your Dad was one of the few survivors of the Stalingrad offensive. This was one of the turning points of the war. The battle was one of the bloodiest in the history of warfare, with combined casualties estimated at nearly two million. When I looked the battle up on Wikipedia, I learned that: *"of the 91,000 German soldiers captured in Stalingrad, only about 5,000 ever returned. (Remarkably, your father was one of those.) Already weakened by disease, starvation and lack of medical care during the encirclement, the soldiers were sent to labor camps all over the Soviet Union, where most of them died of disease (particularly typhus, cold, overwork, mistreatment and malnutrition)."* You explained to me that, as an officer, your father was not supposed to be placed in a labor camp, although at the beginning of his captivity he was. Sometime later he was transferred to a Russian prison camp, and remained a prisoner of war for more than seven years. You recall meeting him at the train when he was finally released. By then you were ten years old and he was a stranger to you. He returned home weighing ninety pounds and never spoke of the war again.

During this same period my family managed to leave Bulgaria, taking no belongings, except for some articles of clothing, two down comforters, and some jewelry. They travelled across many countries to reach Portugal, where my family began the long voyage to America. My father had been able to book passage on one of the few boats still crossing the Atlantic, and I have been told we were some of the last people to be allowed to leave at all. Before reaching Portugal, my parents stopped long enough to have my sister and me baptized by a Congregational minister, and buy two gold crosses that we wore around our necks. The rumors of what was happening in Europe to the Jews frightened my parents enough to make the decision to leave and to try to hide our identity. Everything was uncertain. By then, Bulgaria's king had gone into exile, and the country was occupied by the Germans who used Bulgaria as their breadbasket, as well as a clear route to Greece and Turkey.

Perhaps one year earlier, your family had fled from your home in Silesia moving west to avoid the invading Russian army. Travelling west, you passed through Berlin, witnessing a city in complete ruins. Impressions of war remained vague in your mind, because you were too young to fully understand what was happening. You were able to remember only a few stories about that flight. You were ill with the measles or the chicken pox and running a high fever. You, your mother, and your older sister, also sick, stood on the cold train station platform in the middle of winter, suffering from cold and frostbite, and waited for a train that would take you out of harm's way. You were the one given a warm blanket to keep the chills and fever at bay because you were the youngest and the sickest. But your sister also suffered. You headed west, eventually arriving in the small agricultural town of Rhoden in the Hessian region of west central Germany. Your family was given one room in a stranger's house, refugees in your own country, and you remained in Rhoden till the war was over.

When your father returned, you were able to move to the much larger town of Bad Arolsen only 12 kilometers away, where you lived until your graduation from secondary school. Life in Arolsen was pleasant. While you were never a perfect student, you were a voracious reader, a talented athlete, both tennis and track, a loner in some ways, but always fun loving. You took long bicycle trips to neighboring towns and villages, loved to sing in the town chorus, (years later you could still hum bars from Mozart's Requiem), and you were fond of ballroom dancing.

Your father slipped back into his former role as head of the household, and you discovered he was a good natured, simple man who was able to resume his life with a degree of ease. His fondness for roses was evident in the hundreds of photographs you found after his death, of the roses he grew by his garden. Your mother was more complicated. She was a trained opera singer, but never had a chance to develop a career. Once the war was over, she made a meager living playing the piano at neighboring village functions. Later she worked for a government bureau whose mission was locating lost relatives and family members.

You talked of the occupation by the Americans as a pleasant time, and often remarked that the American soldiers were good to the village children. You remember hearing music in their canteen, and soon fell under the spell of American big band music and jazz, a taste that would stay with you all your life.

Our early history had some common as well as disparate threads. Both our families were refugees and both were running away from an enemy. Our family feared the Germans, and yours, the Russians. The fact that I was Jewish made our eventual union all the more poignant. Since I always viewed you as an individual and not someone attached to a history I had never quite felt a part of, I had no conflicts or predispositions. I think you felt that you were given an opportunity for redemption though you never spoke in those terms. When I told you that my parents would have been pleased to have known you, you were touched and honored. I had no doubt they would have been delighted that we had found each other, and would have enjoyed the bonus of speaking German with you—one of five languages they spoke fluently.

AN IMAGINED ENCOUNTER

Of course we had lives long before we met. And I know that had we met earlier when you were so handsome and I was good looking, we may not have been able to connect. Aside from your being married, we lived such different lives. Once, based on an anecdote you told me, I found myself imagining a scene through the eyes of a camera. As you remember, I often see moments in life in a cinematic way as if they were scenes in a movie. I sometimes see my own life that way. Early in our relationship, as I was getting to know you and the people in your life, it was easy to form visions of your life, so different from my own. As you were telling me a story of driving your friend's bride to her wedding, I began to imagine the following scene—the imaginary first encounter.

EXTERIOR: SECOND AVENUE & 16TH ST., NEW YORK CITY
A car, driving much too fast, approaches an intersection.

ANGLE: CLOSER ON CAR
The Driver DIETER, is a tall rakish man in his late twenties. About to be best man at a wedding, he's dressed in a tuxedo. In the passenger seat is the BRIDE, an attractive young woman, in full bridal whites. The BRIDE is terrified: the MAN is preoccupied. (He is thinking about his own marriage and the complicated circumstance he finds himself in. He has already started drinking, and has probably had a few too many.)

PULL BACK: LONG SHOT OF STREET
A taxi enters the upcoming intersection.

39

ANOTHER ANGLE: CLOSER ON THE DRIVER

Oblivious, he continues to speed into the intersection. At the last possible moment, he suddenly
becomes aware of the cab and violently swerves
(SOUND: Skidding tires, screeching brakes) to
avoid a deadly collision but--

ANOTHER (LONG) SHOT

--not enough to miss the front fender of the cab:

(SOUND: CRASH)

ANOTHER ANGLE

The infuriated CAB DRIVER gets out to check the
damage, hands on hips. A second later, his passenger gets out. She is clearly a smart young woman
in a hurry. About 25, dressed in a mini skirt,
boots, a hip Sassoon haircut, dark glasses. This
is YVETTE. As she hands the driver some bills for
her fare, she glances with a kind of contemptuous
amusement at the bride and the tuxedo, as though
anybody wanting a formal wedding at all is hope-
lessly square.

                    YVETTE
                (to cab driver)
        Sorry about this, but I'm late for an
        appointment.

ANOTHER ANGLE: YVETTE EYEING DIETER

                    YVETTE
                 (mutters)
        Asshole!

ANGLE – DIETER & DRIVER IN FRONT OF DAMAGED CAB.

Surveying the actually minimal damage, DIETER hands a few hundred dollar bills to the cab driver, and then glances up--

A WIDER ANGLE

--at the departing Yvette, just as she turns to look quickly back at the scene. For a split second, their eyes meet. Then just as quickly, she continues on her way, as Dieter turns to go back to his car and the badly-shaken bride.

FADE TO BLACK

So—now they have both seen each other. Their paths have crossed, but for the moment it is over.

I often think about the way lives converge. Parallel mostly, until some circumstance bends their paths to form a crossroad. We met at that crossroad. Had I met you when you first came to this country, we would never have found that bend in the road. We would not have recognized each other. It was meant to happen after a lot more of life had been lived.

A MOUNTAIN ROAD

We were driving through the mountainous country, between Albi and Rieupeyroux. The driver seemed to take no notice that the road was hazardously narrow and twisted and turned like spaghetti. My fists were clenched tightly around an invisible support. Coming directly at us with equal speed, was a car, the "angel of death" about to seal our fate. Time slowed down and I understood my life was likely over. It would be here in this beautiful place, on a quiet mountain road, in the southwest of France. Our driver maneuvered the car, squeezing it into the minute space between the road and the mountain to our right, and, I saw to my astonishment, there was just one breath of space between the two cars. What stood between life and death was a space you could barely pass a needle through. We would survive. From that time until the now aching present, I had assumed that nothing could ever damage the lucky star I lived under.

THE PREDICTION

I told you that long ago I had my horoscope read by an old astrologer, the grandson of Chester Arthur, (one of our undistinguished presidents). Gavin Arthur was an old school Theosophist and lived in one room in a seedy residential hotel in the Tenderloin section of downtown San Francisco. He had drawn up my astrological chart and started reading it aloud as if it were words written on the Holy Grail. In a matter of fifteen minutes, he spun a monologue which was the progression of my life, and I took it down in shorthand, hardly able to digest what he was saying. At some point I took those notes and typed them out and filed them away.

When I met you, all those years later, I remembered those notes and was amazed to find that Gavin Arthur had pinpointed the exact year in which I would meet the love of my life. I remember clearly that when I first read that—back when I was twenty-one—it seemed just plain silly. I would be an old woman by then! But I was the exact age he predicted when I met you. When I told you this, you were delighted and chose to believe that the old man knew exactly what he was talking about. Two years later we were married.

Your sunshine is our clouds and rain storms. The storm today was biblical, and has left me feeling quite blue. Thunder, lightning—a wall of rain that came down without letup hour after hour. My geraniums liked it, though, and the sweet potato vines in my flower boxes are thriving. When the rain let up, I went out onto the deck, hoping to capture some of the magic of the fresh air the rain had left behind. It feels lifeless, even with the humming birds and other song birds flitting about. Sometimes I feel okay. Sometimes it is all unbearable. I can't know what I will be feeling from one minute to the next. I do feel like a broken record. I am a broken record! It is late again, time to go to bed.

It was early in our time together. The move from my post and beam pre-revolutionary house, where I had lived for over twenty years, to your marvelous mill with open spaces and enormous windows, was a series of slow and deliberate steps. First came the computer. Then the two cats, and on this Sunday in late winter, it was time to get the sixteen Toulouse geese from my barnyard and transfer them to your mill pond, along with the paddle boat. We cornered the geese and one by one put them in burlap sacks as gently as possible. They ran honking, with wings outspread, from one corner of my large yard to the other. Sometimes we gathered them on the run. After a number of hours, we managed to get them down to the car, on which we had already strapped the bulky paddle boat. As we drove the five miles to the Mill, I held the boat steady with one arm out the window, and you wondered out loud, what the cop would think when he stopped us, which we had no doubt he would do. We arrived without incident, took the paddle boat down to the pond, and then began to release the geese. I was sure that they would be delighted with their new home and their own pond. But they flew in every direction, onto the front lawn, into the ravine near the waterfall, downstream, and gone from sight. We were able to gather some, and the others returned on their own, but I fretted endlessly, checking on their whereabouts by the hour. Each morning I tried to coax them up to the pond, but they would not budge. I took the long climb down the ravine and back up again to shovel snow out of the way and put down feed. I loved you for being so willing to accept and nurture my fondness for wildlife. I remember how deeply you felt the death of two of the geese who'd been mangled by dogs, and how you walked directly up to the owners of the dogs and told them in no uncertain terms that this

47

could not happen again, ever! You held me close and comforted me. You stayed in it with me.

ROOTLESS

Pine trees are known to have shallow roots. As they grow taller and heavier, a strong wind can easily blow them down. I have something in common with pine trees. My roots have never grown deeply. They have formed tendrils that spread along the surface in wide and uneven ways, but have never quite taken hold of anything that made me feel grounded. I have moved along the periphery, occasionally joining in experiences that had the feel of connectedness, though in time seemed to fray, unravel, and lose their grip. In this way, I feel we were very much alike, Dieter. You loved your home but knew you could leave it in an instant. You were not tied to anything. You considered spending time on a freighter, stopping from port to port, without caring much about ever finding one place that couldn't be replaced. Restarting was always a possibility. You were a nomad, or so you called yourself. Even though your life appeared grounded and stable, you could chuck it all, replacing it with a completely new experience, without ever looking back. We both felt we were loosely wired to wherever we were. The absence of place began early for me, with feelings of alienation. Though I was barely old enough to perceive the difference, I attribute my sense of displacement, my not wanting or needing to be part of anything, to the fact that the land of my birth was not the land in which I grew up. You moved away from where you were born, driven by a spirit that you felt deeply. It was inspiring to feel this kind of portability, the sense of movement, because we were together, the wire that connected us was all we needed.

After your death I was given a book of poetry, *Wild Geese* by Mary

48

Oliver. She expresses what I feel but cannot say quite as well. I read it over and over again. Her words resonate. She instructs the reader to do three things; love what is mortal, hold that love firmly, but when the time comes, let it go.

NEGOTIATIONS

This chapter of my life began with the drama of one terrible and irrevocable phone call, heralding that our life just changed. A one hundred and eighty degree turn. I spent nights awake, frightened, wondering, mostly denying, sometimes assuming that my world would not change. A miracle would dissipate the ominous cloud that hung over us. It would take years to digest the fact that there might be a death in the future. The moments of hoping that your condition would not profoundly affect our lives were stronger than the reality of what had been forecast. We continued to spend time in the company of friends, hiding the deterioration that was observed daily, nostalgic for what we had taken for granted, finding ourselves still speaking in the future tense, constructing plans to override the forced changes we were both going through. For a long time, I continued to believe you could recover. I had a fundamental belief that I was immune from having bad things happen to me or to you, convinced this could not be my life. Everything would return to normal. I began to live in the world of barely being, barely holding on, barely recognizing myself or you. I would reincarnate myself into different roles, grabbing onto daydreams that would comfort me and transport me away from this moment. I sometimes imagined my life without you, romantically viewing it as an opportunity. Nothing really worked. It was just the various tricks I was playing on myself.

A grief without a pang, void, dark, and drear,
A stifled, drowsy, unimpassioned grief,
Which finds no natural outlet, no relief,
In word, or sigh, or tear -
       Dejection: An Ode, Samuel Taylor Coleridge

Thinking in a quiet place makes one's thoughts vividly loud. My thoughts stream in, without censorship. The phrase, "authentic spirit" keeps playing in my mind. What is an authentic spirit? Am I thinking of you? I probably am. Then I hear another phrase: "Hiding one's light under a bushel." Or is it a bag or a bush? I don't know! Was I doing that? I realize that for the first time in my life I was content to live behind the spotlight, because I knew I powered that light. The spotlight was aimed at you, and I was happy to take in its warmth. I had no need to impress. You had my back and that was enough.

I am wondering if it is possible to ever get close to someone new. Some people are wise enough to think it through ahead of time. I have to hit the wall head on, bruised and bloodied, before I can figure it out. From nowhere, I hear a voice within me say: "Mother, can you see me? Mother, what do you think? You died ahead of any of us. Do you understand more than I do? Would you tell me to calm down and take my time? Would you tell me that everything will be revealed one day? Are you saying that what we think we know and feel is not necessarily what is?" Okay, I think I get that, but I'll make a note of it anyway. Then there is faith. I find myself wondering about faith. What is it, and how do we adopt it? Can we actually just have it, and is it available on command? How do we find it? Is the need to survive just primal and instinctive? Do we have any control at all?

Thoughts continue to stream in like run-on sentences. Now I begin to contemplate the nature of friendship. I feel forced to think about this. I reckon it is important. But I can't quite figure it out. I find I am redefining what friendship is. I think it must be a powerful thing. The next thing I hear in the tide pool of my mind is: "It is just a fleeting thing...."

51

THE WHITE CHINA CUPS

This morning I picked up one of the three white china cups that are left. We had used those cups for eighteen years. I do love them. They have a lovely shape with scalloped edges, but no frills, are delicate yet robust. I, who tend eventually to break anything within reach, have kept them safe from myself. I have handled them with care because they served as a fragile link to our European beginnings. They have been my symbol and daydream of a gentler world I chose to imagine was real.

The day you lost your balance trying to bring them back to the kitchen, in a desperate effort to be helpful, was a marker on the road we found ourselves on. A vivid reminder of the whittling away of our life. I helplessly watched one of the cups slip out of your hands, fall to the floor, and break into pieces. I swept them up and tried to speak calmly as though it did not matter. It was just a small, unimportant accident, but you understood, and there was not much I could say to comfort you or make a difference, because we both knew that this was another sign of things to come. Oh, I did love your hands, how you handled everything with surety and care, your grip firm. They were articulate, and showed how gracefully you had used them. One was not surprised at the beautiful things that came from them.

THE HARDEST THING

This is the hardest thing I have ever lived through. It has been a long time, not as long as some, but still it feels an eternity since my life was normal. I can hardly remember when I was not sitting in the waiting room of one medical facility or another—leafing through magazines or blindly watching television while I waited for you to get out of surgery, or radiation, or chemotherapy, or an imaging center, or when I was not

53

visiting one doctor or another with you, or picking you up when you fell, or having to inject you with medication twice a day, or trying to get you in and out of the car, wondering if I would be able to.

Still there have been some small joys throughout this ordeal. Times when it still seemed possible to experience a day together and imagine a future when this nightmare would only be a memory. But lately, as the end seems to be scripted, those small joys have vanished, and it feels like I will never be able to laugh again.

LETTER TO FRIENDS - APRIL 25

We were told on the thirteenth of April that Dieter's treatments were not helping. With some hesitation we asked the doctor what we could expect. No more than another three to six months. The doctor said he was sorry. I wondered how often in any given day he had to make that announcement. Since then, Dieter's decline has been more dramatic than I could have imagined. He hasn't much strength at all. He can no longer turn himself from side to side in bed. I am sure I am witnessing the last phase of his life. In order to make his life as comfortable as possible, the den has been set up as a sort of hospital. He will nod, in appreciation, rather than speak, when anything is done for him. The person we have all known has changed completely. There was a short time, not so long ago, when he rallied and was able to work, although even then, for considerably shorter periods of time. But he was independent. After October, the frustrating side effects of the treatment caused him pain due to hematomas forming in his knee and leg, but still he could walk on his own, though his balance was impaired. By March the signs of his mind losing ground were becoming more evident, though I could not admit it. The steady movement downhill began in earnest. I wish for a miraculous recovery, but know that the chances are slim to none. He is resigned to death. My efforts to mitigate the circumstances are meager. I keep fresh flowers, cut from the garden, by his bed. The house is filled with music. Keeping him comfortable is my only mission. No attempt will be made to keep him alive any longer than necessary. In so many ways he has already left us. I am without hope but resigned. At least I believe I am. I do not want him to linger a minute longer than he has to.

DIFFERENT RHYTHMS

You called my name as you raced up the stairs, two at a time. *"What,"* I remember thinking, *"do you want now?"*, mildly irritated because of the distraction. I knew you were about to make a suggestion that would alter the course of what I was doing. I remember that I sometimes felt reluctant. Breaking my concentration often frustrated me. Now I wish for nothing more than to see your sawdust-tinged face as you rushed into my office with that enthusiastic, boyish way you had about you when you found the need to break up your day, suggesting a perfectly good excuse to carve out a pleasant distraction. You would sense that I wasn't always as eager as you were—but I always stopped myself from just saying no, realizing even then that life is short and spontaneity, golden, particularly when both our rhythms could be incorporated into the day. I would always be glad that you forced me out of myself. Moments I now wish I had the power to play back again and again.

A STRING OF BEADS

Visualize a string of beautiful beads, each bead slightly different in color, shape and design. They have been chosen carefully and work together to make a statement. Some shine brighter than others, catching the light and dazzling the eye. A few are smooth and translucent, others abstract and opaque, individual beads securely held together with a strong but flexible string. If the string frays and breaks, they become merely individual beads, tumbling to the floor, rolling away, getting lost under a couch or behind a divan, small things you can trip over. My life feels like a broken necklace. Occasionally, I find one bead and it temporarily delights me, but the rest are either lost or very hard to find.

LETTER TO A FRIEND - MAY 28

Dieter is returning from the hospital today. Now that he is bedridden, he may not be so difficult to take care of. Friends, two or three that I can count on, may come on some afternoons. I don't know how long Dieter will linger in this state, but I can tell you that I am hoping it is not too long. I may have entered the deepest part of the grief process because I can't imagine feeling much worse.

Young women come to bathe him and take care of his most intimate needs. They are younger than a daughter of mine might be, hardly old enough to understand what this is all about. This is their job and they want to do it well, so they are cheerful. As they stand by his bedside, looking down at him, they speak loudly and chatter about things that seem so trivial to me. They say, it has been a really nice day, or wonder if it will ever stop raining. They won't be here tomorrow, because they have the day off, and yes, they will visit their boyfriends' families. They plan to get married right after graduation, which is just a month away. What, I wonder, does Dieter think of all this? Is he wondering how he got here, and who these strangers are that are taking care of him in ways that up till now were his private tasks? I do not leave when they are there. I need to help them, to assure Dieter that I am still here and will not abandon him. I feel a need to protect his dignity. I need them to understand that he is my husband, the man I cherish. What they see is not the man I have spent so many years with. It is not how he should be remembered. This alteration is only temporary. Though these may be his last moments, this cannot change the fact that he once stood upright, healthy and remarkable, and I am the witness and the beneficiary of his life. But he does not complain, rather he thanks them as they are leaving.

LETTER TO YOUR SISTER - MAY 31

We had the most terrifying thunderstorm today. The rain came down as if the heavens had truly opened up, the thunder sounded like cannons, and the lightening was close and continuous, lasting most of the day. It is just now starting to lighten up.

This vigil is taking a toll on me. I make meager attempts at making my life tolerable—I breathe deeply, exercise, meditate, even pray, but it is like lighting tiny candles to illuminate a vast space which has no light at all. There is no sound emanating from his bed except the drone of the motor that keeps his mattress inflated. It is not possible to go very far without needing to be right back at his side. I am weary and have given myself permission to stop trying to convince people that I am fine. I am not good company. The sun did come out yesterday when friends came for lunch, though there was still a threat of rain.

LETTER TO A FRIEND - JUNE 4

I feel as if life is only happening outside my windows. I watch the cars go by and think how the people all have some place to go. School busses are picking up children. The bakery is open and beginning to fill up with the usual crowd. Women are gathering on the porch to play Mah Jong, a guitar player has arrived from North Carolina, and others from Louisiana, all sitting on the porch steps of my friend's house. One of this mixture of troubadours is singing absent-mindedly, while others are strumming their guitars and fiddles. As I work in my friend's house, her dining room table my desk, I am aware that life is going on, but I am an observer, not a participant. I am the one who waits, not part of anything, going through the motions, but not quite able to be there. This is a special time for me, lonelier than a hollow tree.

In the past few days I have not been as distraught as I had been previously. Perhaps this terrible nightmare has become more daily, and I am not fighting the truth of it. But I do need to take one day at a time. Little things set me off and pull me down—like walking into his workshop and realizing he will never again design or make furniture. Or seeing his shoes in the closet, a vivid reminder of the certainty: he will never need to wear them again. The finality of his illness and his impending death sinks slowly in. I don't know what death feels like yet. I don't know what being gone forever really means. In some impenetrable way, death is an abstraction. One can't see it. He finds moments to say something wry about his circumstance, so he is still very much aware of what has happened to him. But those are slivers of consciousness. The always-present Dieter is no longer really here. I perform the rituals required when tending to the sick. I keep up a dialogue with him, often he cannot follow it, and I find I am praying that his time is drawing down. I find this process hateful. I am not so attached to life that I feel it should go on no matter what. There will be relief and anguish in equal measure when his life finally comes to an end. I believe, but am not sure, that I am prepared for this. I have come to terms with death over the past months, and while my grief is intense, I am ready, and I know he is too. He has accepted the reality of his incapacity, and his mind has allowed him to drift past that knowledge so it does not hurt so much. I can find no anger building yet. Right now it is all ritual and the gestures feel shatteringly insignificant.

My energy is easily drained—my heart has been fractured. Life is surreal. I am losing Dieter. There isn't much left of that wonderful human being—he has had enough, and now he waits patiently for what will come. When I sit with him, he says, "And how are you? Where do we have to go today?" He does not recognize that he cannot even carry his own weight. He no longer has the ability to stand. I say quietly that we have nowhere to go. We can stay here for the rest of the day. He just says, "Oh." And then he is silent. When I take care of him, he implores me not to work so hard—and then he is quiet again. He listens to music and stares at the ceiling. I ask him if he would like to read. He sometimes says yes, but mostly he blinks his eyes indicating that he is fine. And one day melts into another. I wake in the morning, after a restless night and tiptoe to his bed to confirm that he is still breathing—that his life still continues. Then the day, the same as the day before, begins all over again

THE EARRINGS

The capacity for spontaneity and determination was part of the complex individual that you were. At the same time, you would always counter that you were a simple man and that was true too. In remembering various moments, one in particular makes me smile because it demonstrated so much of who you were. You had the ability to remember the smallest things when it came to pleasing me. I must have mentioned in conversation, when it turned to the subject of jewelry, that I did love large gold hoop earrings. Rather than the round tubular gold ones, I imagined that square cut gold hoops might be elegant, although at the time, I had never seen what I had in mind. You ordered a pair when you stopped in a jewelry store somewhere in Massachusetts, and discovered they existed and could be ordered. Just a day before Christmas Eve, as you were trying to get the last piece of furniture you'd completed ready for delivery, you got a call saying the earrings could be picked up.

Normally with a delivery of furniture pending, you would not allow yourself to be distracted. On this day, you drove two hours to pick up the earrings, came back, loaded the furniture into the waiting truck, and drove two more hours to install it. It was a very long day. But the joy you felt at presenting me my gift on Christmas Eve seemed worth it to you. When I wear these earrings, which are the only ones I do wear, I remember how you always made me feel special. And how in turn, that awareness allowed me to know how special you were.

GLIOMA

I believe I am observing the first stage of the end of your journey. You sleep deeply and continuously for hours. The cancer makes it impossible for you to have meaningful conversations anymore, a fact that is still hard to grasp, remembering that you were known for your wild, uniquely contemplative conversations. What is the nature of this particular cancer which they call Glioma? Glee-om-ah. It does not have the sound of something bad. It almost sounds like a mantra. But it is nasty. It congregates in clusters and then splits apart and forms tiny armies of enemy cells that wander and glom onto whatever is in their path and cannot be captured or eradicated. They split off forming new pathways in expectation of doing further damage.

I read all I could about your condition. Parts of me would have liked to have kept it a secret from myself. Even as I read about the deadly nature of this viral type of cancer, for a long time I thought you would survive, against all odds, that it was simply too soon for you to leave, and that I would never have to be witness to this day. Glee-om-ah!

But you are peaceful. One might almost use the word "sweet." Your true nature is most prominent now. It allows you to have a certain calmness and lack of fear, which demonstrates your basic nature with such clarity. I am almost happy when I see the sun, because this entire spring has been cold and wet. I actually don't mind the rain, as I have nowhere to go and couldn't leave you anyway. But when the sun streams through the windows, it makes our rooms look brighter. I often think that when it is raining, the skies are crying for you too.

NEVER FREE OF NOT KNOWING

Friends feel sorry for me. I can tell. But there is no need, as I am doing such a good job of feeling sorry for myself. You still speak to me, but your voice is hardly audible and I cannot hear your words. I can only see that your lips are moving. You look so sad, and I sense you are saying that you are so sorry for having put me through this.

What I want to say to you is that today I am able to remember vividly the happiness that you have brought to my life. Strangely you and I were cut from the same cloth, and I can barely think of a time when we were not in accord in all the time I have been with you. I want to say how much I came to rely on you—as my best friend, my lover, and confidant. I want to remind you that the strength you gave me is now being called on and needs to be made actionable as I face the challenge of life without you. I want to say that you are home, and it is the only place I want you to be. Being here to tend your needs means everything to me. The importance to me of your being at home outweighs the downsides, and the downsides are many. I am never free of not knowing, while you are focused on the place to which you have been summoned.

So live that when thy summons comes to join
The innumerable caravan which moves
To that mysterious realm, where each shall take
His chamber in the silent halls of death,
Thou go not, like the quarry-slave at night,
Scourged to his dungeon, but, sustained and soothed
By an unfaltering trust, approach thy grave
Like one who wraps the drapery of his couch
About him, and lies down to pleasant dreams
　　" Thanatopsis" Williams Cullen Bryant

HOSPICE

The peonies are gone now. The cherry and the apple trees are blooming. We are now beginning to see the renewal of life.   I am so grateful that so many people care about you. The contrast of life outside and the rapidly diminishing life force inside these walls, is palpable. That force speaks to me so strongly now, while the litany of each day has not changed. Hospice has taken over a good part of your care. The team of professionals who are taking care of you impress me with their sensitivity, care, and quiet assurance. This is the way to die. Your death is imminent. It could happen tonight or weeks from now—it is just not knowable.

I speak to you when you wake, whispering to let go because I know you do not like where you are, and when you were a well man could never have imagined yourself in this situation. You wouldn't have believed you could tolerate it. Yet, you are patient now. Your legs are skeletal, and your arms grow smaller every day. There is barely any muscle left. You still have a firm grasp with one of your hands. You maintain your gentlemanly demeanor, greeting the aides politely and wishing them a good day. But your voice is now a whisper. That is the state of things. I feel as though I am on a roller coaster whose speed has been slowed down, but I cannot seem to get off. You are leaving an inch at a time. Occasionally I see a hint of a smile. I take you out of bed for breakfast, and direct you to the familiar place you have always sat in. You tire within the hour, so I hoist you back to bed. For the rest of the day you are asleep with an occasional period of waking. Interest in food has diminished. I know that when you do not want food at all, the end will be near. I know this is what you want. I have been in a state of grief for so long now I can hardly imagine any other way to be.

THE TABLECLOTH

Last evening, another gathering of those who have been our friends. A familiar setting and you were there, or your words were, stitched into the tablecloth where, through the years, we had been invited to write how we felt about the wonderful hospitality of that home. The two of us were present in at least three places on that cloth, spanning so many years. The hostess has painstakingly embroidered our sentiments, and our familiar handwriting has been carefully affixed with cotton thread into the fabric of that white cloth. There was one from 2006, October, and two other comments from other times. Evidence that you were here. You were a genuine part of people's lives. I found that exhilarating. So many evenings spent here. Loving words spoken. Pleasant conversations. You would have been in the middle of it. I admit that I drank a little too much wine tonight, as I rarely do these days, and I felt my spirits loosen and I could speak with animation, and you will be glad to know that for a little while I felt just a little like the person I used to be.

HOUSEPLANTS

The Bird of Paradise, a plant so large you could wrap a newborn baby in its extravagant leaves, was always one of the most dramatic plants in our collection. That towering plant is now a clump of dead stalks. The Ficus Benjamina or weeping fig, inhabiting an entire corner of the living room, is weeping abundantly and most of its leaves lie on the floor. The Sentry Palm ranks high as the best palm for indoor use and it promises to last indefinitely. Its large feathery arching leaves, once so full, are no longer there. It did not survive. I am losing so many of our houseplants. It is both curious and troubling. I have had them for years. They have always produced new leaves in the right season, verdant, healthy and strong, doubling the space they first took up in the house.

Now they are one by one failing. I tend to them conscientiously, exercising an important part of my nature. I never forgot my duty to keep them properly watered, and fed. I painstakingly clean their leaves, repotting them as they outgrow their containers, and change their location to suit their requirements for sun or shade. Watching them flourish was important to me. Some of the spirit of life must have left the house, and now they are informing me that they require more than I am able to give. I seem to have lost my healing hands. These living things which have always created beauty and a kind of permanence in this house, are one by one drooping, dropping their leaves, and turning brown, and I do not have the capacity to revive them.

LETTER TO YOUR SISTER - JUNE 29

When the television is on, Dieter watches and makes comments mixed together in a maelstrom of diverse thoughts and memories no longer attached to time but plucked from the fragments of his mind. I cannot follow him. I used to correct or explain, but I see that it doesn't make a difference. Then he is mostly quiet. We are visited by friends, who come in hopes of comforting us, but in their eyes I see the sadness and disbelief, as they try and cloak their sorrow in friendly chatter. He stares at them, trying to participate, and mumbles softly to acknowledge their presence. He follows me with his eyes. They take me aside and wonder how I am holding up. I feel their discomfort and sadness—viewing a friend as he disappears before their eyes. I find myself smiling wistfully, knowing what this must look like. I brace myself to prevent the tears from welling up. I shield myself from the possibility of being pitied.

BREAKFAST WITH THE BIRDS

Remember our mornings at the mill and breakfast? It was our ritual for all the years we had together. The beginning of another day. A favorite time. In the early days it started with the sound of birdsong, the standard opening of Robert J. Lurtsema's radio program, *Morning Pro Musica* on WGBH. He started his programs that way, right up to the time of his death. For a while after his death, his program continued, including the Sunday morning Bach cantata countdown. Inevitably, though, the programming changed, the music was gone, and with it the birdsong, except for the sounds coming from the birds nesting in the ivy outside our window. We brought our coffee and light breakfast to the table in the living room by the window. Those quiet moments prepared us for the day ahead. We did not want to rush into that other world, which would come soon enough. I have not continued this ritual.

SOMETHING WORTH KNOWING

A bit like purgatory right now, stuff to deal with, and then the waiting. I cut a beautiful rose from the bush outside the door and placed it near your bed where you can see it. Music plays softly in the background. I am happy when the sun shines through the windows. I imagine you may like it too, though you do not say. I am alone most of the time and feel very dull. Laundry every day, cleaning up, making beds, taking care of your needs. You implore me to take a rest. I tell you that I am fine, and, yes, I do get out once in awhile. I toss off your concern and tell you I am just pecking away at busy work. Sometimes, when you are asleep, I pick a task that will satisfy my need for industry, such as polishing the brass candlesticks, which leads to setting my sights onto larger tasks as I attack the refrigerator or the stove. There is some satisfaction in making things shine, making them look new again. It makes me feel as though I am stepping out of the room of pain in which I live. Then a phone call— actually quite a few. How am I doing? I no longer know what to say. So I simply repeat myself. I try to read, but never turn the page. Have I emphasized how much I need to keep busy and how dreadfully long the days are? I believe I have. I write letters to you, things I can no longer talk over with you, chronicling my experience. Something must come out of all this pain, something worth knowing.

LETTER TO MY SISTER - JULY 2

Time is endless—like walking through a long tunnel that just keeps going. There is no hope of anything good happening, and not knowing when the end will come is just plain hard. I sometimes forget what life was like when Dieter was whole and full of life and energy—his deep voice, for instance, is gone. I do remember all the things about him—but

68

they are fading. I haven't seen him upright and walking for a very long time. What was his smile like? It has been such a long time since Dieter was part of all I knew. Even with people calling and coming around, and Dieter right here, I am lonely, for him, for us, for what our life was. There are moments when I don't think I can stand it. My patience is thin.

PSYCHIC STEPS

I found the perfect mate in the middle years of my life. You championed my every move and appreciated most everything I did. You recognized and celebrated my capacities which gave me courage, clarity, and purpose. I no longer cared nearly so much about all the little imperfections of my character, because you convinced me that who I was, was more than enough and you would always love me. You confirmed that every day. I probably didn't tell you how much I loved you. Not nearly as many times as you felt free to tell me. But you were content in the knowledge that I did and knew without my having to say it, that you were the single most important person in my life, beside my son, and that I would never do you harm. Did I prove that to you in those treacherous last months of your life? I worry about that.

Your condition prompted rages in me that were uncontrollable. My fear and concern made me maniacal. There were times my fear took the shape of anger, when I realized you no longer resembled the man I had known all those years, and, selfishly, I feared that you were leaving me. The loneliness that greeted me every day in the last year of your life was so painful that I simply had to ignore the terror of getting up in the morning to face another day of exile. My eyes could see no further than the blank and staring gaze of a tomorrow that held no promise. The essential thing that drove me was the reality that I had to be ready for whatever the day would bring. I tried to reassure myself that I had a life. What I was actually doing was emotionally putting everything on hold. I hoped that I would soon follow you. I was both burdened and strengthened by the position I found myself in. I had to feel that you could rely on me. I had to trust that I wouldn't fold, precisely because I was holding up both our lives when so much was at stake. Did you understand that as you were moving farther away, I was being pushed closer and closer to the understanding that both of our lives rested on my shoulders? Part of every day was spent sitting beside you, sometimes silently, sometimes talking to you, often without hope of a response. I would try to ignore you. By concentrating on the minutiae of errands and tasks that we normally do without much thought, and by trying to complete the tasks necessary to maintain our circumstances, I allowed myself to avoid focusing on the room where you slept. I tried to find comfort in the urgency of what I was doing, so that I could, for that moment, forget the harsh reality of what was happening to you and to me. I felt surer of myself when you were asleep. I often hoped you would not wake up.

As I write this, I realize that despite how much I felt you had changed, you were still dearer to me than I can describe. Time has passed since those terrible days. And as it does, I realize that saying goodbye to the world I had known and cherished involved many psychic steps. It required an ability to step aside and see things from a separate place. I had a need to focus on a small clear crystal ball, a single day and a single task and nothing else. I found myself trying to deny yesterday, not worry about tomorrow, and concentrate on that one day.

THE TEACHER

I wonder if we would think differently about death if we were not so fraught with feelings of loss and abstractions. It may be our most instructive teacher. It is Socratic and experiential, teaching us to confront existence by asking questions, and finally accepting the sheer unpredictability of life. Perhaps we are like a marching band, changing formation, or groups of lemmings, drawn to the abyss, dropping off the ledge and disappearing, as if we were never here. Those in the procession are a diverse group, travelling together. One by one the group grows smaller. All we have known begins to fade, and in its place the next group begins its march to the edge, and on and on for all time. My circle is shrinking. What I also visualize is the forming of a vortex which eventually swallows the memory of our place in this universe, sweeping us away, so the next and future souls will be allowed their chance to expand. Maybe religion grew and prospered because it offered explanations and reasons so that we might remain content. In my view, we are just borrowers of a piece of time called life. I suppose religion helps to soften the much too difficult notion that this collection of days may be all we get.

THE LUDDITE

You often said that when you retired you would learn to use the computer, but you found many reasons to avoid getting even mildly acquainted with it. Whenever I tried to introduce you to it, you gallantly paid attention for a short while, then just shook your head and said it was a puzzle. You hoped there would never be a time when you would have to depend on one. Technology had no real place in your life. You could make a complicated piece of furniture. You didn't see why you should use a computer when you could draw free hand a piece of furniture in perfect perspective, while speaking to your clients. A gentleman from another era, you felt comfortable in the civility of a former time, and so, for all your intelligence, you could not, would not, join the rest of the crowd in the 21st century. You would often say," I need to get off this planet." It did not strike me as powerfully then as it does now. It may explain why knowing you were dying did not distress you. You accepted that the new ways were foreign to you and hoped you would never have to adjust to them. You were proud when you called yourself a Luddite and had no plans to change. So in some sense it is fitting your time on earth has come to an end, before everything you had grown accustomed to-changed.

SHUTTING DOWN

Oh damn, I am in a deep new low. You have been asleep since eleven o'clock yesterday morning! Loud noises and lights go unnoticed. You are not yet in a coma—but you are shutting down. I have thought this before, but this is real now. I feel there are still parts of you that understand what is going on—and you are just waiting and wanting the end to come. I remain calm but what is not possible to control is my own deep sense of loss. I can't shake that. The fear of what happens next is always there, but for right now I just wait. I visited your bedside many times last night—I cannot sleep. How many ways are there to say good-bye?

THE SECRET

I keep constantly changing photographs of you on my computer desktop so that images of you are never far from view. The pictures are from other times and so many other places. You are always looking straight at me with your keen and straightforward look. I have photographs of you just days before your death that I cannot put on the screen. They contradict the memory I must retain of you. I prefer to hold on to the images I remember best: a handsome man, talented, assured, hard-working but able to relax.

The other pictures that I keep stored away, but do look at from time to time, show me the sorrow of the end of your life—the quiet helpless stare of someone no longer truly present descending towards a place I cannot know. I try to find in those pictures the essence of that crossing. I scrutinize them to see if you are telling me how we begin to end our life on earth. This kind of scrutiny is difficult, as I am emotionally unable to break away from what I understand, to move along with you on your journey. So what remains is the sound of a beat, which is probably my heart, and my eyes which can only see in these photographs that now there is a secret you cannot share.

FORGIVE ME

Dieter, I am haunted by the memories of the past two years. I don't know how to think about them. How do I judge my actions in the morbid reality of what would be your last months on earth? I thank the power of chance that you would have me to look after you till the end.

At the same time I remember thinking I am the one to be left behind. I often wondered how I would end my days, but brushed those thoughts from my mind, knowing there was time to think about that later. I looked over at the bottle of morphine, momentarily comforted by the thought that my life might not have to be endured. My job was to make you know, even in your weakness, you were loved, and my only task was to take care of you. That mantra was continuous. I must be strong, I must not waiver. Sometimes I did lose the strength of patience and shouted at you for falling, for getting up hour after hour. I would have to be there to be sure you did not fall. I hated having to play your nursemaid. I hated that you needed me to. I mostly hated that this was happening. I would have to dress you because you could not. I hoped you would understand and forgive me for my frustration. I would say, I am sorry for all the things I have to perform in order for you to get through one day. For having to convince you that the injections I administered twice a day into your already bruised abdomen would somehow keep you alive. Mostly you remained steady. Sometimes you would become slightly annoyed with my attempts at helping you, and push me away saying, "I can do this, I can dress myself," and then feel defeated when you could not. I would ask your forgiveness for not being stronger. How far away did you find yourself from me before you took your last breath? While you slept, I began to steel myself for the inevitable, and found myself doing things to prepare myself for the moment. I thought about just what I wanted to say to everyone who mattered when the time finally came. I thought endlessly about how I would present the news of your death. I designed and redesigned the announcement of your death, weeks before the event, leaving out only the actual date. I did this to make myself believe I was in control.

I will not know if you knew the terror I was feeling as I took your temperature on that last day, alarmed that it continued to spike higher by the hour. I vaguely remember putting cold compresses on your neck in an attempt to keep you from overheating. Did you hear my heart beating and notice how my hands began to tremble? I knew this might be the last of your days. Did you hear me whisper, as I lay my head on your chest—as close as I could be—so you might hear me say that I wanted you to let go. I know you worried about me. Was this even a concern of yours anymore? I still refused to admit what I knew was true, and in denial, allowed myself to leave you that evening. All the facts were there, but I was not ready to face them. Did I know that evening would be your last hours? I believe I did. I will always wonder how I could have left you. The vigil, I now realize, was just too painful. I needed to be elsewhere for just a little while. I thought you would wait for me till I returned.

When the friend who was staying with you that night came to the door, I had to only look at his face to know the simple fact that you had died. I knew as he was saying it that this is what I expected. Walking over to your bedside, I looked at you, and asked how you could die on this particular night when I was not with you. When night after night, day upon day, I had been there. Yet I was not witness to your last breath. Did you wait till I was safely gone? Was it your intention that this would be your last act of kindness towards me? I continue to roll this question in my mind like a scroll. But I did leave you on this particular night. It was a Friday, the tenth of July. It was 2009. You departed sometime around 10 PM. I recall that as I sat in the theater at just about the hour of your expiration, I experienced a sharp pain and gasped. I believe firmly it was then that you took your last earthly breath.

After the hours of waiting, and finally finding myself alone, unable to get to sleep, I knew it was time to tell those who cared the final news. It was too early to use the phone, and I wouldn't have had the courage to talk to anyone. So my message was sent out through cyber space, knowing how strongly you would have objected to this. It was a simple message. There seemed nothing more I could say;

Subject: Dieter is Gone

Dieter died last night (Friday) at 10:15 PM. He slipped into death quietly, and as peacefully as he had accepted his illness, so did he accept his death. He took my heart with him when he left but I am forever grateful that we were together for the time we had.

I know that allowing you to die at home was important. You were in the place you loved the most. I remembered that you would stand in the middle of the large room and arbitrarily, for no good reason, declare, apropos of nothing at all, that you loved this place. And it was in this place we experienced our life together. It was the place that we seemed destined to be, and it was right here where we were happy most every day. It was in this place, holding within its walls, some new and difficult memories, that you began your new journey—leaving me behind to wave you on your way. This may be the time to thank you for being in my life, making it so rich and perfect. Can you hear me at all? You were a romantic—but not nostalgic or particularly sentimental, so I feel sure you will find a way to tell me when my grief becomes a burden to you. Your pragmatism was manifest in so many ways, and yet you were touched by many things. I recall seeing tears in your eyes when you thought about the holocaust, or learned that an acquaintance you liked very much had a promising child who died of an overdose in a college dormitory room. You will let me know, perhaps insist, that I allow light to enter my life once again. You will let me know just when that will be, won't you?

A KIND OF EULOGY

You were comfortable living within the boundaries of your conclusion. Boundaries you created for yourself and felt comfortable staying within. Life was a mystery that could not be solved, so you found a way to make life about what you recognized was important to you. You defined those elements that made life and how you lived it worthwhile. You were enthusiastic in the same way that you were fatalistic. But you were satisfied that where you were was the place best suited for who you believed you were. You found it unnecessary to harbor vengeful thoughts, preferring to keep feelings like hate out of your life as inappropriate and harmful, while you kept your energy directed at the positive things in life and lived by the standards you created for yourself. When we joined our lives together, we were ready and able to live life fully, content because we had come to know each other when the pressures that often consume a marriage seemed to have disappeared and we were enveloped in a loving alliance. We were still young enough to want to explore and experience new adventures, and able to enjoy a personal independence that made our lives abundant and whole. I was the wife who not only experienced the joy of a perfect union, but the one handed the privilege and the accompanying heartache that allowed me to see you through your life's final challenge.

A few days after your death, I found myself in a peculiar state of mind. I opened your clothing drawers and all your closets, emptying out the contents. Among them, there were only a few things I wished to keep. You always chose your clothes with care, and shopping for new ones came only out of real necessity. The inventory was limited, but what you owned was high in quality and in perfect condition, except perhaps for the tuxedo which you still wore after almost forty years! Moths had eaten through the fancy lapels so it was not hard to give up.

I placed the rest of your clothes in countless plastic bags, stuffing them with what was left of you. I worked ruthlessly, a bit possessed, until I came to your shoes. I remember you most vividly when I recall your leather shoes. You wore sneakers only when you played tennis. For a tall man your feet looked lovely in shoes. They were so tidy and you chose them with such care—often waiting till we were in Germany to buy them. You had some for nearly thirty years. Only the ones you worked in had to be replaced more often, as you walked miles in them and they were covered in sawdust and lacquer. I took each pair out, one by one, placing them in rows on the floor, and on the rungs of a ladder which I had set up to reach the upper closet compartments. You would never again walk in them. They were now all on display—gaping, feetless shoes. Watching this silent parade I broke down completely. Some time passed before the breathless sobs that gripped me began to subside. I sat at the edge of the bed muttering and wailing. I hurriedly gathered up the shoes and stuffed them into the waiting plastic bags, hurling one after the other into my car, taking them to the nearest Salvation Army bin, tossing each bag, one after the other, as quickly as I could, before I could change my mind. Of course I did not give up everything. A few of your possessions couldn't be given to strangers. I hoped a particular friend would take a few of your shirts, a sweater and a pair of boots he always borrowed when he came to visit, and most particularly the silk paisley and cashmere scarf that I bought you so many years ago. Home again in the still early morning, I remained in this state of frenetic industry for most of the day. Standing in our bedroom, where I could no longer sleep, I focused my attention on the rest of the house. Impulsively, I decided to rearrange it. I am certain I hadn't showered or brushed my teeth yet, but remember that I did manage to pull on a pair of jeans and a tee shirt earlier in the day, and in this state, I rearranged all the furniture. My intention was not to make the rooms look better but to make them look different. In the midst of this chaos there was a knock on the door.

A neighbor who lived a mile down the street had come to call. He was a well preserved man who, at age eighty-eight, had come to offer his condolences. I was in such a solitary state of mind that good manners had left me, and I remained planted at the entranceway as he began to tell me how sorry he was. I clumsily accepted his kindness, without the presence of mind to invite him into the apartment. My home was a private and terrible sanctuary which had enveloped me in grief and I was unable to share the space with anyone. But he had come with a purpose and walked down the stairs looking sad and spent because his own wife was ill and in a nursing home. I knew he was lonely in his aging and solitude. I wondered later that I hadn't had the grace to offer even the slightest degree of civility. That I had failed to recognize that he might have liked to sit awhile over a cup of tea and commiserate on the turn of events that had left both of us emotionally disabled. Many months have passed since then. I still agonize over the memory of that visit.

AND THEN THERE WAS ONE

Driving to the airport to pick up my son, I am aware of how unwelcoming the night time is for me. I haven't actually told you yet, Dieter, that my son is coming back and will live in the building. The fact is, his return feels like a divine twist of fate and completely unexpected. His presence, I am sure, will allow me to make what was, and still is, a hard and rocky time, just a little easier. But even his presence can only soften the hard edge of my sadness.

It still takes a real push for me to get up and get out. I find the short days hateful. I am aware how much you added to my sense of freedom and the capacity to embrace life. You were my partner and companion, so nothing seemed out of reach. The reality is that I am now travelling by myself. While I knew this condition before I ever met you, the years we were together changed my view of the world. Now I have to redefine myself, relearn and negotiate as an individual. I am tied to nothing.

People seem to naturally want to pair off. I recognize that these pairings are often less than ideal, but it is a natural state for most. We seem drawn towards finding comfort with another person. That these pairings do not always produce perfect comfort is the theme played out in courts, and in literature. But for us, it was perfect, and so I now feel a poverty pervading much of what I do.

Every day brings some small recalculation of what interests me, what harbors I might explore, what can be gained in a narrower channel, and still the deprivation is palpable. I must greet friends by myself. I am now the one left who must open the door to let people in.

ASHES TO ASHES

I speak with you every day and I write down some of what is on my mind. Sometimes the smallest things bring you back to me. These are the memories permanently stored, though there is no stone or marker to visit. Your remains arrived in a black box in a plain white shiny shopping bag. You rested on the wooden filing cabinet you had made for me. You sat there for over a month, waiting for your birthday and your memorial service before we finally would release you. I took that black box, heavy with your ashes, to a spot by the stream behind our home, accompanied by the three people who mattered most to us—my son, your best friend, and my niece. The ashes floated down the stream, where I emptied your remains into the flowing water the day after the memorial service. You were now only fine dust.

I suddenly had an odd flashback to my meeting with the undertaker (is that what he was?) Whatever he was, he was a proper man, wearing a dark suit—poorly fitted—who had a strange way of saying things with a studied reverence. His voice had a mechanical and droning quality. He arrived the day after your death, and wrote down the answers to the questions he needed to ask, telling me what to do, what they would do, and ended the session holding my check for $1400 which is how much it cost to turn you to ash. And some time later he called again, saying, "May I bring the cremate back to you?" The *cremate*! You were no longer referred to by name. You had become a noun. He brought you back to me in a box inside a shopping bag. The box had a label with your name and the number: 11607. You sat on my filing cabinet for weeks, and later, I placed you on the cherry table for the memorial service, flanked by sunflowers. The next day I poured you into the stream, in the area behind the house that we called the meditation grove. And as I did this, you filled the stream with the color of cloudy champagne. You drifted away, taking your time, forming beautiful shapes—almost mesmerizing—till, finally, you drifted away to join the gurgling brook—except some of you clung to a round rock near the bank, where you remained for weeks and weeks.

TALKING TO THE DEAD

These letters to you are my attempt at telling you what is in my heart and how I am seeing things now and how I am getting on. I wish I could have chronicled you better. I don't have the words this minute to draw you in a way that brings you to life. I am not entirely sure what this exercise is about, but somehow I know I must do it. I still talk to you all the time, but I get no response, and yet I believe, magically, you must still be near, because what I cannot reconcile is that I will never see you again. But there remains the telltale signs of your presence manifest in so many ways. In the furniture you built and the photographs of you. These are my assurances that you were not just a dream. That we did share a life, and that life was once beautiful. The floorboards I walk on now are the same ones you stepped on. Your fingerprints are everywhere. I have abandoned our bed though. The last months of your life, tied to that bed, bring back only terrible memories.

ADRIFT

I stand in our living room with the sun streaming through our windows. The room has changed a little, and our breakfast table sits against a different wall. I rarely sit here anymore. I am hardly ever in this room.

Today is Saturday, and I am adrift and don't have any ideas or energy with which to conduct this day. Mostly I wander about, pacing in our sunny living room. The English call it a lounge, but there has been little lounging going on. On this bright Saturday in February, I am feeling so much the lack of you. Seven months have gone by. Nothing makes much of a difference. I find myself watching television as if that will change my mood. At first, before I become distracted, I feel there is still life outside these walls. Spokesmen are still hawking products and there are people who might actually want them. Then I notice I am still in my slippers. The breakfast dishes have yet to be washed. I can't work up the energy to spring out of the doldrums that come to me often these days. They are particularly strong today. I am missing you more intensely today than some days, but realize that sometimes the feeling isn't as powerful, which leads me to believe that I may be over the worst of it. Then, unexpectedly I am awash in a torrent of longing. I don't know why there are so many variations in this endless task of learning how to be a widow. Today, in particular, I cannot reconcile the fact that you are not, nor will you ever be again. I cannot pretend that if I am more active, care more about life, do more, reach out, think seriously about anything, become involved in something, this ache will go away. How can I feel so dramatically sad? It is personal and I cannot give it away. It belongs entirely to me. It is some-thing unwanted which has glommed onto me and I am unable to remove it. You showed up in my life. You lit it, and then, the light dimmed and went out.

GRIEF

The word that surrounds me is grief. It has become more than a word. It has become a live thing, infiltrating everything, like water. Grief has the capacity to rearrange itself and accommodate any space or object, attach itself to whatever you are doing. It is everywhere, and it is not benign. When, out of desperation, you light a cigarette, it combines with the smoke. When you slip into your jeans, it surrounds your legs. It mingles with the smell of coffee grounds, sits on the steering wheel of your car. Stares back at you in the mirror. When you run, it joins you. You try to pound it into the ground, only to find it has grabbed onto your toes. It mixes in with the sound of a word or phrase and takes it for its own. It follows you when you make the beds and has a place of honor on your pillow. It is my special, but unwanted, companion.

PROMPTS

Occasional prompts really set me off. Today, I was in your shop. It has the look of an interrupted moment, and suddenly I had the sensation that I entered a time warp in which at any moment I will witness a burst of activity. The lights turned on, announcing the day's work has begun. Then each machine is on, creating the loud perpetual din I am so accustomed to. You will be cutting wood for your next assignment or installing hardware on a wall unit slated for delivery. I can almost hear my footsteps as I walk into your office, and as I look around the now still room, I hear your powerful voice speaking on the phone—articulate and unique. A momentary lapse in time, and then I see you leaning over your desk, surrounded by sawdust, working on a drawing. I look again, shift my eyes and realize that everything is dark. Everything is silent. Your ghostly image sends spasms of grief through me.

MORTALITY, IMPERMANENCE, CHANGE

Looking at an advertisement in a magazine, I see the picture of a tall man whose back is turned to the camera so that what is visible is a youthful yet mature man who is tall, slim, and casually dressed. He is leaning against the door of a fabulous garage, looking at a classic, restored, antique car. The picture describes the story of a successful man, with the luxury to ponder over the restoration of a beautiful car, surrounded by the winnings of his successful and happy life. I spend time looking at the photograph, realizing I am unable to accommodate the motives of the advertiser, whose message is: "This could be you!" The photograph was designed to tempt me into purchasing something. Beguiling me to dream that this could be my life and in that way, lure me into believing that this gentleman would be able to enjoy his fortune from this day forward and always—and naturally, so would I.

I realize I will never again aspire to anything like that, knowing I am no longer in the expanding and acquisitive part of life. I have an urge to contract, at least in the material sense, and I know for certain that life does not go on forever, and that material things have only a fleeting value.

I understand fully that I cannot stop the process of life. It takes the death of the most important person in your life to start you down this path. I find it interesting that my mother's and father's deaths marked the beginning of the sobering realization that I was moving towards the front of the train. But I took that in stride. I was sad about their passing, but I could accept their deaths as the natural consequence of life. It felt oddly reasonable. Your death, Dieter, does not feel reasonable—although that is not logical. In the aftermath of your departure, I find myself looking at everybody and almost everything in a new way. There is a growing understanding of the impermanence of all things. Not much seems important or finds a place in my life, and I am confronted by the reality that we are a race of mortals, each with a death date we will have to keep. Up till now I would not allow myself to think too seriously about that. It might make life too unbearable. But now I understand that life, in order to continue, must include death.

WATCHING FROM MY WINDOW

The wind is howling and the snow is coming down full force. I am alone with my son's four dogs in the house which feels almost eerie. Sounds reverberate through the walls, windows squeal, the roof creaks and yawns under the weight of the snow. It brings to mind past snow storms and winter days when we were together. It reminds me of how often you would not heed my real fear of driving during a snow storm. You did not mind such inconvenience, not fearing the slippery roads, or the lack of visibility, or other drivers who could not control their cars. Most snow storms would not deter you from your plans. You regarded my fear with surprise, but would not let that interfere with whatever it was you felt you had to do. I remember feeling somewhat angry that you found my cautionary attitude silly, and yet you would sometimes agree that it was not a good idea to travel and your better sense would keep you home. Then the storm could rage and I was at ease. The white cover that blanketed the landscape would feel magical. Now, as I look out at this white night, I shiver and smile and know you are safe.

THE TOUCHABLE MARK

I receive so many written tributes about you from people whose houses are full of your furniture. You have left that mark. I suppose we all leave something, but even for the most remarkable of us, that memory is swiftly erased by time. The furniture you have designed and made are concrete marks that will last longer. The mark may become anonymous. It may, and probably will, become dated, though some will be passed on to the next generation. Some will be hacked apart or sold for timber or used as fire wood. But by and large you have created environments that will linger in the souls of those who live in them and in that way, you will, through your furniture, be witness to the timeless roll of life. I am aware of that here in "our" home. I pass by your furniture and often stroke it, hoping to get a sense of your life force within each of the pieces. I stroke the door of the wardrobe that I have always admired. I hold my cheek close to the door and find myself saying, "Good morning, Dieter."

PREPARATION AND TRANSFORMATION

Dieter, you won't believe the changes that have taken place now that my son has moved into the Mill. The showroom is now his apartment. Your workshop, a garage! So though I am still facing the challenges of living alone, I am no longer living in unending silence. I now hear the scraping of paws and the occasional barking from his pack of dogs, bringing much needed life to the upstairs of this building. There are new voices and a new energy permeating the premises. You will be relieved, and pleased, I think, that change has begun to sprout, and with it the sense that this building and its grounds will continue to be looked after and valued.

The most difficult change, however, was the dismantling of your downstairs workshop, the place that held the strongest memory of your spirit. The picture of all those hammers and screwdrivers, trim saws, and orbital sanders lying in various places, waiting to be used, glue drying where it had spilled, notes and sketches on the worktable, used sandpaper, and sawdust in great mounds around the belt sander and the table saw. The jointer's reverberating sound along with the gnawing screech of the shaper, the sound of men's voices just above the noise of those machines—all are now silenced, and the other smaller tools that turned wood into fine furniture are gone. We had to dismantle it entirely. You can imagine what a painful and arduous task that was. The years of sawdust have now been vacuumed away. The debris that represented the hundreds of pieces of furniture that were made here—thrown away. It is now completely clean and empty, and has become a place where only cars are parked. The disappearance of your essence is tangible and emphasizes the transition I must make if I am to get on with my life. Upstairs where we lived has also changed. I have given away many things.

There is a need to have less. But the last piece of furniture you made, as you were finding it harder and harder to work, is the prettiest of all, and I have kept it. A wall unit of natural cherry with many drawers and doors perfectly proportioned and trimmed with black hardware that contrasts beautifully with the soft color of the wood. This one holds special meaning for me, because we both knew it would be your last.

THE RING

I remember surprising you the day we celebrated our fourth anniversary. The fact is we actually had two anniversaries, the anniversary of our marriage and the anniversary of our first day together, which we recreated and celebrated each year, except for the last two years of your life, because by then you were far too frail. You died four days before that anniversary. When I say anniversary, I always think of that first "date" which started with brunch followed by an afternoon at the Tennis Hall of Fame. The matches always fell on or near Bastille Day, July 14th, so for all our life together that is the day we celebrated our anniversary. I often had to be reminded of the date of our wedding, even though our wedding was not less memorable, but we wished it to be more like a party than a wedding, and we did not exchange rings. I believe we both felt that formalizing our union was enough, but four years later, as we were waiting for the matches to begin, we wandered into a jewelry store where I saw a plain wedding band that I liked and realized then that I did want to have that symbol on my finger. You were surprised, and wondered why I had never asked before. Until I saw that ring in the case, I hadn't considered it. I also wondered why I hadn't.

I think about you most strongly as I am waking and when I finally allow myself to go to sleep. Your picture is by my side. I put off going to bed as long as I can. One would imagine it would be the opposite, that in sleep one might lose oneself, might escape the empty place. And yet, finding no comfort in sleep, I cling to the day in the hope that I will not have to repeat the cycle all over again. Still, the mornings often bring a sense of newness, and as I wake there are random waking dreams of you. This morning what came to me was—driving. You often said that being a truck driver would have suited you, as you never seemed to tire of being on the move. You were good at it too. You also talked about race car driving, which might have been your passion had you given in to that urge. For those who drove with you, there was sometimes a sense of screaming fear. You drove that fast. But you were sure behind the wheel, and attentive. You were able to drive for hours without a break. Your trajectory was always forward, and you didn't like to stop. When you were sick, I let you drive because once behind the wheel, you seemed to regain your balance. Eventually it was no longer safe, so I took over the job of driving. When you told me that I was driving well, I felt I'd been given the Pope's blessing.

The two times we traveled through the southwest to California were oases of singular joy for both of us. We found ourselves dreaming wildly, the landscapes were so large they could accommodate our most expansive notions. There were many such journeys—from Quebec to South Carolina, from Colorado to California—from Paris to Aix en Provence and through the Luberon—travelling along the River Mosel and into Paris. We travelled most often by car, and you were often at the wheel. But things have changed. I have become the sole driver and I still hear your instructions when I am on the road. Never drink or eat while driving. Keep both hands on the wheel. Do not slow down while passing a car. Always pass on the left. Remember the trailer truck's blind spot. Do not make phone calls, and never pay attention to well-meaning drivers who signal you to go ahead into an intersection with a flagrant disregard for whatever else might be happening on the road. Ignore those well meaning drivers at all cost, and always, always drive beyond the speed limit!

THE CHAIR

The pair of big brown leather chairs holds memories that should be lovely, not the least of which was the joy in finding them. They embrace you, steady you, hold you up and comfort you when you sink into the protection of their massive embrace. I find myself sitting in one of them, staring blankly into the large room, turning my eyes toward the other one. It is empty. I have been in my chair for hours and cannot move. My mind is empty too. Occasionally I turn my head—the only part of my body that seems to want to move—to look at the other, trying with the strength of my will to superimpose your image, fully alive, and place you there. The harder I try, the emptier it stays. You will not appear. My eyes move up towards the ceiling, a blank canvas on which I begin to project images of the two of us. The pictures appear slowly, one by one, but soon come faster and faster like the years spinning out of control, until they become a blur. Huge drops of water dampen my hands, clasped in front of my eyes. I realize I am screaming.

Why does the body cry? What makes the body shiver when it cries? What is being released that can no longer be contained? Is there an endless supply of tears? Can you run out of them? Maybe I will run out, dry up—and if this happens, will the pain dry up too?

THE DREAM

Last night I had a disturbing dream. I felt as though I were waiting for something—but didn't know what it was. Eventually our car pulled in to the driveway. I knew you were in it, but I couldn't see you. I looked furtively through the window, knowing that I must have let you drive alone, and probably should not have. Another car pulled in right behind ours. I saw you, or thought I saw you, in the driver's seat, and felt some relief. Then I looked again, and realized it was not you, but a stranger with a beard. You were in the passenger seat, slumped over and completely naked. The driver said he saw you on the road driving erratically and managed to get you over to the side of the road. Somehow all your clothes were gone. He took the wheel of our car while his friend followed in their car. I felt a sinking feeling seeing you brought so low. This was the first and last time I have had a bad dream about you. It woke me up and stayed with me for hours. It was not hard to interpret. It was right there before me. The vulnerability in which you had to live all those months before you finally made your exit. Naked, weak, and at the mercy of your caretakers. You remained silent and accepted these conditions, but I knew inside you felt that whatever we did, however much we tried, it was useless, and out of kindness and patience you simply accommodated us.

There is motion. There are cycles. But for me there are simply long days that resemble each other. One follows the other, and then they become weeks. It goes on. The process is slow. The drama is subtle. My emotions go through extremes. The swing from one end of the spectrum to the other is staggering. Sometimes I am robotic, sometimes frenetic, sometimes merely calm and philosophical. I am aware of people who are truly caring and present. They are there in a variety of ways. I need to refuel, because I am out of gas. I am blind and deaf and unable to figure out how to negotiate this road. My face is brave, but my heart feels as if it has simply stopped. Will I manage to get through this experience intact? I do not know. It is, after all, just life: beginnings and endings. We seem to be less prepared for endings. Certainly I am. What I am hoping for is that I will come through this with more than I imagine, that I will be able to get through this first year without you.

SHORT DAYS OF WINTER

This is the time of year when night comes much too soon. The winter days are short and the transition to nighttime unsettling. Twilight. I have never liked this time of day. It always feels like what I imagine purgatory to be. The ill-defined transition from one time to another, in a light that is always melancholy. More so these days as I do not have the comfort of your presence to make me feel there is someone special I can share the onset of night with. This is a dark and difficult season. The lights are strung on many of the houses up and down the street. I am thankful for this custom. It helps to light up the night. I imagine there are crowds of people in places where I will not be, who are thinking of what they will give, and what they will cook, who they will share this season with, and all the ways they invent to make the season come to life. For me, Christmas was about traditional things. I looked to Sweden and England to form a notion of what I would like to trim the holiday with. When you came into my life, the spirit of Christmas was renewed and I was happy to participate. Darkness comes early these days, always difficult, now more than ever.

THE PITS OF TARTURUS

I am in a peculiar state of mind, a kind of desperate indolence. I am a shriveled leaf losing form and shape, landing on a pile of disintegrating humus. I have joined the legions of the fragile. So many days of my life are spent without uttering a word, and I am frightened. I feel I could fall down a rabbit hole with just a gentle push or, worse, be tossed straight down, if it were not for small tasks or obligations that mark the hour of the day and the days of the week, that get me outside of myself and keep me connected and allow me to wander without getting lost. A point

103

of reference that forces me to participate in events that will satisfy the requirements of work. I pull myself out of my silence to make phone calls at appointed times, to support others in their own journey towards health. Calls in which I become the voice of hope, allowing me to focus on someone other than myself, and understand the real and difficult conditions others find themselves in. This sharing of information, coaching others back to health, keeps me temporarily from my own sense of loss. And by charging myself with tasks, like sweeping the stairs, or polishing the mirrors, or dusting the windowsills, I do just enough so my environment does not betray the devastation that I am feeling. Perhaps I can hold it all together. When I am able to follow this regimen, I feel I have achieved a great deal. But if there is no structure, no schedule to maintain, nothing written on the calendar, no dinner with friends, I lose all sense of time, and one day follows another without clear definition. I am agitated that I have allowed the day to slip past me as it abruptly comes to an end without my participation. I am aware it does not belong to me, and wonder if I will ever again feel a surge of energy that had in the past been my guiding spirit.

Can I simply order myself to find enthusiasm and avail myself of what is offered? Will I ever have the desire to embrace life, and will anything ever capture my imagination or fascinate me again? Can I hope to take pleasure in birdsong again, or the sound of water rushing over stones. May I anticipate the day when I wake up knowing that I have returned?

RISING ANGER

Everything I do, whatever I feel, however much I obsess about this or that or anything, all are merely expressions of something that is missing. They seem to occur because you are not here. I am confessing something to you now that I could not have believed I could feel. There is a rising anger overwhelming me. I am putting myself through this maw because you are no longer here. None of my unhappiness would exist if you hadn't left the room. All my requirements and dreams would be satisfied and I would not be left to wander in this foreign landscape. You have left me no future. The past is now just a painful reminder of what I had. The present is without hope of believing anything will satisfy the reason for getting up in the morning. My life stands still. I have been abandoned.

CHAMPAGNE ENDING

There is something mildly romantic yet shocking in taking your own life. Churches condemn suicide, hotlines try to prevent it, and psychiatrists get wealthy trying to explain it. For some it is an escape route, the thought of which provides comfort. A notion that we can have a hand in our own destiny. It is the word spoken in hushed and furtive whispers. Institutions tell us that taking one's life is a sin, that it must not be an option. Often it is considered an act of cowardice or desperation, and the assumption is made that one would have to be in a very dark, depressed, possibly deranged reality to consider it. The pain must be so unbearable that escape requires the harshest and most troubling act of all. But I am not convinced. I wonder if it could not be a final act of independence and courage. Why, I find myself asking, are we trained to accept that our life must end naturally? Are we breaking with some cosmic pattern? Must we remain alive because of the high value placed on life? At the same time, life's natural ending has been pushed away by the intervention of medical wizardry. Is it not justifiable to consider, through our own calculations, that the quality of life as we personally define it, may simply not be worth continuing?

WHAT IS THE COLOR OF DESPAIR?

On any given day, I will meet people who are aware of our ordeal, now my ordeal. Not all were friends, present in our daily lives, but were certainly acquaintances. I meet them in various ways, and they do ask with real sincerity about how I am doing. I always say, I am all right, thank you. And they are content. They can continue with the sense that they have said what is expected, expressed the act of caring, and the activity that brought us together is allowed to continue. And each time I say that I am all right, I know that is all I can say. To convey what has happened and what I am experiencing requires a power of words that I cannot always express or would want to intrude into other people's lives. I suspect that those who are going through this very same loss will have different layers of feelings, not necessarily the same as mine but equally hard to explain. What, I muse, is the color of despair? It is not black, for there would be no light. And there is light. It would not be gray, for that is too bland to explain the sense of what has happened. It is certainly not yellow, for that color radiates warmth and cheerfulness. Perhaps despair is icy white, emitting an unearthly glow as the memory of every moment simple and profound shines lifelessly. What was is there, yet it is not. It is an essence, so it is untouchable. Fragments of memories no longer come back to life in strong colors, lost in the icy white of forever being without you. Those fragments blur, disappear, then reappear as if a gauzy curtain has been blown open by the wind.

Permanently gone are your long striding steps through your large shop. You will never again sit on the deck at dusk with your book, your cigarette and your gin and ice, enjoying the rustling of the trees, the bird songs, happy to watch the day pass into evening. Never again will you be found in the chair at your desk making phone calls and writing checks, grumbling at how quickly the money is spent, while you sketch out what you will need to get ready for the next day's work. There is no next day. Permanently missing are your comments about the day's news or life's little ironies. No longer present is that whole-hearted laughter that brought tears to your eyes. Extinguished is your energy to do whatever was necessary. Knowing how to be calm when there was nothing much that could be done. And permanently absent are the Sunday mornings when you dressed for the day, putting your blue jeans and work sweater aside for a clean shirt and cords. You will not be driving to the bakery listening to a Bach cantata on the radio, and there is no more need to fetch two glazed doughnuts and the Sunday paper. No longer is it possible to sit beside you when we drive to wherever we have to go. Vanished is the companionship that was the heartbeat of my life. And it is permanent now that I will never see you again. Each of these everyday memories produces in me a contraction of the heart that takes my breath away and leaves me with a sense of such profound loss that it is unspeakable. Yet, I do feel ungrateful at times.

I find myself comparing my life to others, all around the globe, wondering that I can be so self-absorbed when others have lost their homes, their families, their limbs, and are living in fear and perhaps starvation. Their loss is greater than my own, their pain far more intense. I grieve for them too, yet it does not change what I am personally going through. I wonder if my pain is diminished by the greater pain in the world in all its manifestations. Beyond natural disasters there are the conscious acts of human beings willing to destroy life for a purpose that is flawed, idealistic, and evil. It is beyond the realm of my understanding and it makes me wonder if earth is indeed the hell that is spoken of. There seems to be nothing holy about living. Yet selfishly, that is what I wish for. Your magical return to the living.

THE SADDEST PICTURE OF ALL

It was a Sunday and friends came to have breakfast with us. Other friends were visiting for the weekend. Pictures were taken. Those pictures tell me so much of where in the decline you were. I think it was hard for me to make the comparison generally, but the photographs tell me what I was still unable to grasp. In one photo, you looked lost. Listening to the conversation, you had a faraway look which makes me wonder if you were even there. Another photograph shows you staring into the camera and this photograph haunts me because there was nothing in your eyes that was familiar. In fact they were dull and almost menacing. This was the day you whispered to me that your mother was there, and though, even as you said that, you knew it could not be true, you were convinced that you had seen her. The supernatural was imposing itself on the daily reality. I remembered being told that as death comes closer, it is not uncommon to begin to see people from your past who are no longer living. It was on this day, sometime in early May, that reality once again confirmed what I continually confronted but was unable to fully comprehend. Parts of you had begun the journey away from the world we understand. You had gone to another place that is not recordable. You had passed over into that realm which you could not speak of, because whatever you were experiencing was locked deep inside of you, and we, on the outside, were witness only to what we could explain. The mysteries of the mind go unrecorded because those who are in another place do not have the words to describe it. That place must have a different language entirely, a personal language known only to those who are in transit.

LIFE IS A SERIES OF EPISODES

You often described life as a series of episodes, some connected, some not, arriving with no explanation and no way of knowing how they would conclude, each framed in the way most stories are constructed. I have to come to terms with the reality that your illness and subsequent death was, as you would express it, just another episode, and that there are future episodes to explore. But some are played with just a few instruments, in a minor key, while others are scores so profound they require a full orchestra.

My mind is in a fury to capture every single moment of your life as I knew it. As in Bradbury's Fahrenheit 451, I want to place in memory all the moments and gestures that made up our lives, to be able to call them out whenever I need to. That might be my way of keeping you alive. Perhaps if I try hard enough, I can make those memories float across the water like a barge, so they are strong enough to walk on. For it seems to me that our lives are not made up of the dramatic moments, but rather all the small yet significant ways we spent each day:

> *These beauteous forms,*
> *Through a long absence, have not been to me*
> *As is a landscape to a blind man's eye:*
> *But oft, in lonely rooms, and 'mid the din of towns and cities,*
> *I have owed to them*
> *In hours of weariness, sensations sweet*
> *Felt in the blood, and felt along the heart;*
> *And passing even into my purer mind,*
> *With tranquil restoration: —feelings too*
> *Of unremembered pleasure: such perhaps,*
> *As have no slight or trivial influence*
> *On that best portion of a good man's life,*
> *His little, nameless, unremembered acts*
> *of kindness and love."*
>
> *Tintern Abbey, Wordsworth*

I do not want to lose the memory of your voice. I sometimes still hear you answering the phone, your familiar response to the question always asked, "How are you?" to which you would always say, "Fine, yourself?" I could always count on that. I can see you sitting over a cup of coffee, reading the newspaper, often using your teeth to manicure your nail…the funny way you had of brushing away hair (no longer there) from your forehead when you were about to say something you had spent some time thinking about…the way you would sometimes play with words and construct sentences so long that even you couldn't remember where you had begun. Then there are clear visions of how at ease you were, relaxed but mildly formal, when you met new clients. I remember how you were always able to charm potential customers with your manner, competence, and confidence. I still remember how, returning home from a day away, you always greeted me with open arms, an enormous hug, and a kiss that was minutes long.

If liquid was spilt on a tablecloth you were beside yourself, yet your car and your office were coated with sawdust. If a rug was not angled correctly or a painting askew, you felt obliged to straighten it out immediately. Dishes were not left in the sink. Clothes were put away. Eventually you learned how I felt about your bed-making skills, and you kindly left that to me. You made fun of me for ironing the sheets, but you were amused rather than rude. And after years of living with you, I became sensitized to the disease you called "deliveritis." It always showed up the day before, and of, a furniture delivery. It was often an anxious time for you and involved a long evening of work to complete the project. I learned to let you go through your paces and stayed clear of you, knowing when you returned home after your piece had been installed that you would cheerfully stride into the room and with satisfaction, say, "Well, we are much richer today than we were yesterday," fold yourself into a chair and feel for the moment, satisfied. I remember that you always walked through your shop with long, steady, rapid steps. I never saw you saunter while working. You were able to relax completely once your work was done. Inherent in your makeup was the ability to prioritize your day. And perhaps the single most remarkable characteristic was your ability not to worry. You knew, with certainty, that if nothing could be done at that precise moment, there was no need to ruin a perfectly good evening and a fine glass of single malt Scotch.

THE INVISIBLE VIRTUAL WORLD

I am hanging tentatively on the periphery. Life feels murky and unclear. I am able to gather myself together and give myself rules which I often break. I pass through each day, and start again, managing to accomplish at least one of the ten things that I have listed as urgent. The days tick on. I am getting closer to the one year mark, the anniversary of your death. I see the variations my daily life has taken and the different moods that accompany me. Sometimes I am present. Mostly I am somewhere else. I feel restless and undisciplined, thrashing about, compulsively moving into a virtual world. I find myself needing to talk to strangers, to comment on their lives, the condition of life in general, or anything at all. The outside world comes in through the window screen of my computer, a whole new world of people saying things that often leave me unimpressed. I enter these social networks whenever I wish to. I boldly write what I think. I am able to do this because I am protected and invisible. I am only a username. I know they do not know me and I do not really want them to. It's a far cry from being truly known. It is important to remind myself that while I am now invisible, it was not always so. One person in this world saw me, loved me with all his heart, fully, genuinely and unselfishly. That is no small thing.

As you drifted in and out of my mind, today, I began to feel for the first time a sort of dread. As if a dense fog has descended and covered all the real memories of the living person you had been. Could I actually be forgetting you? I mean the memory of how you felt, and how you smelled, and how you sounded—how it was to be with you? That thought was more frightening and sadder than all the moments throughout last year when you were dying and I felt like a shadow. More terrible than remembering the last breath you took. I always thought there would be more.

But as time passes, I find myself developing new habits counter to how we used to do things—and I am allowing it. I no longer have a fixed regimen. I do not watch the news at six. I go to bed impossibly late, and often forget to make dinner. I drink coffee standing by the kitchen window, looking out at the waterfall. That is when I panic and believe I am forgetting you. The realization puzzles and scares me, until I understand that I cannot be, because I am still thinking about you, encountering you in so many ways throughout each and every day.

Yesterday, I pulled a document out of a file, and there in the corner of the page, I saw your bold handwriting. A note you had jotted down. It stared back at me, as if it were alive. I ran my fingers over the words, hoping to feel your spirit, thinking about how when you wrote that you were alive. When you wrote that simple note neither of us could have suspected that the countdown towards the end of your life had already begun. That note gave me another way of looking at time. Time is an abstract reality. I find my thoughts reflected in Wordsworth's poem;

Surprised by joy—impatient as the wind

I turned to share the transport—Oh! with whom

But Thee, deep buried in the silent tomb

That spot which no vicissitude can find?

Love, faithful love, recalled thee to my mind—

But how could I forget thee? Through what power,

Even for the least division of an hour,

Have I been beguiled as to be blind

To my most grievous loss!—That thought's return

Was the worst pang that sorrow ever bore,

Save one, one only, when I stood forlorn,

Knowing my heart's best treasure was no more.

That neither present time, nor years unborn

Could to my sight that heavenly face restore.

William Wordsworth

IS IT REALLY THAT SIMPLE?

I sometimes wonder if there is an easier truth for people who live life simply. While I may perceive their lives as boring and unaware, they do not find it so. Their lives feel not only right, but indeed, rewarding. Have they learned to live comfortably in this world because they have no need to ask many questions? They regale me with stories of daily life; what schedule a child keeps, which bathrooms need to be repainted, saying almost in the same sentence and in the same tone that a relative's husband has finally died, having suffered many years from a debilitating disease, and upon his death, his widow is happily free to pursue all the things that she could not do while she tended to her ailing husband. She travels now and does what she wants. And I wonder: Is that it? Is it really that simple? Has the widow been set free? Are exhilaration and a sense of freedom experienced in the dark hours of the morning? Should we conclude that life is a series of duties and freedom from duties? I wonder whether the now-free widow is truly free, or just spending time. Do we, I wonder, pay attention to how we conduct our lives? Whether the method of understanding any of our experiences can be rearranged differently? I ponder the various ways we go through life. It does seem simpler to be pragmatic. An ability to accept change, as if life is just something one does, like removing your hat, or wearing a pair of earrings. It concerns me that the degree to which we view life as precious is elusive. It is an undeniable fact that we covet the notion of life as being a precious thing. What is probably true is that while we say that all life is precious, what we actually believe, but cannot admit, is that some lives are, while others are not. It is the concept of life that is touted as precious. The idea of life. Death is a tragedy no matter when it comes and to whom, unless we are not personally involved. But when it comes to our door, I believe it forces us to redirect our focus. Is our achievement measured in how many times we paint the bathroom or diligently make our beds each morning? Do we conduct our daily life while ignoring its real requests? When death touches us, we become acquainted with another way of thinking and are bound by new rules and conclusions. It seems to me, life is then neither pragmatic nor simple.

I am participating in life, but barely present. Last weekend, I was participating in a conference in Philadelphia; the last two, I'd gone to with you. It was a professional obligation and I had every reason to be there. But in the hotel when the seminars were over and there were no more meetings to attend, notes to be taken, or presentations to be made, I found myself in a bubble I could not break out of. I could not easily participate in the social requirements, though I did make an effort and was able to gather enough interest to make some connections. But even though I certainly belonged there, I was on the periphery of the experience and couldn't get through to a place of outwardly giving. I was able to have lunch with some of my family who lived there. That time became an oasis of familiarity and warmth that enabled me to gain a sense of connection. Then there was an award I received for my work, which I know would have made you proud. And while I was surprised and pleased, it meant very little to me because I felt so detached—as if I were viewing myself as an outside observer or a camera recording the movements of a character who was poorly defined. Going through the motion, yet not really there. I find myself inching my way towards the door, always stepping away.

RETRACING OLD ROUTES

All the roads I travel and all the places I go are familiar because the two of us passed this way many times before. I continue to go down all these roads, to all the beaches, the forest walks, the restaurants, and all the towns and stores we frequented together. These jaunts and excursions have not stopped. Always present in my mind, though, are thoughts of our having once been here or there together. The familiar images continue even while your absence is palpable. Nearly ten months have passed, and I become more forlorn in different ways each day. The hard edge of loss is gone, but in its place there remains my own unconquerable sadness. The fact is, I never expected our lives together to end. Or when it did, I assumed our story would end at the same time. I never envisioned life without you. Sometimes I entertain the thought that you left in the nick of time, still at the top of your game, before the difficulties of growing old could take hold. But now I find the days are no longer mine. I am pulled, as if by a towline, from hour to hour. I am tired. I am always tired.

NO JOY YET

I am bedeviled by an ache that up till now has not been present. For so long I was only willing to hope for safety. I imagined I would find that quiet place within myself, where I could live an ascetic life surrounded by books, good deeds, garden flowers, meditation and good friends. I imagined myself meandering through the quiet turf I called home. I would age gracefully and quietly. Handsome in an old woman way, still able to have a smile that could light up my face as I focused from time to time on the outside world. And people would say, "My, she must have been good looking once." I would learn to love my solitude and continue to write my essays and thoughts and occasional stories. I would meditate and feel calm. And then one day, I would discover the illness that would take me and I would be ready. That is what I wanted and thought would be my life. But at the moment I am feeling restless and nostalgic for the life I had before. All those years have now slipped past and I am left with memories which are not always able to sustain me. Years, some of them wasted—because of the folly of the young, impervious to the notion of growing old, assuming there is infinite time for everything. I resist being cast in the role of someone no longer viable. A woman whose best years are now behind her. Foolishly, I do not want to grow old. I do not want to be overwhelmed by fatigue or hopelessness. I would prefer that my skin have tone and not resemble paper or become flaccid under the force of gravity. I want what I cannot have and this desire brings with it a kind of fury. Perhaps I am just having a moment. These thoughts will pass. I will come to my senses. But while these thoughts germinate, I find them harsh, untamed and lamentable.

This morning I awoke just before dawn. I prepared a cup of coffee, turned up the heat a notch, and crawled back to bed to read. I was distracted, my eyes wandering to the window where there was a faint red glow on the horizon. I remembered your saying, *red sky at night, sailors delight, red sky in the morning, sailor's warning*. I turned back to my book and then once again looked towards the window, and there, through that wonderful large window, I saw the sky grow red—not just above the horizon but throughout the sky. I was struck by its beauty and suddenly felt as though my life might actually have purpose.

I like the room in which I now sleep because, as I am lying in bed, the sky is always present and changing. It has been said by others, and I find it true for myself, that sunrise is the most perfect part of the day. There is a sense then of promise. In these moments, a warm canopy surrounds me. I allow myself to nestle in my featherbed and do not think of paying bills or washing floors. This time is empty of chores and mundane thoughts, and right now I am not even thinking of you. I am not missing you quite as much. I am serene for a few brief moments. It is a pure sensation and I am comfortable. I think of Ovid's description of Chaos: "the world was formed from a rude and indigested mass. No sun was lighted up, no moon did yet her blunted horns renew, nor yet was Earth suspended in the sky." I am here, millenniums later, an inhabitant of this planet, and see the sun as the most vibrant thing. It sails away from the horizon quickly and the day lights up. The transitory moments pass quickly as I try to embrace them.

THE SKUNK

I woke up some time in the early morning hours to the distinctive odor of skunk. When confronted with some yet-to-be-explained phenomenon, I construct a story as I visualize an explanation in my mind. A woodland animal, a skunk, in its slow and nearsighted way, is attempting to cross a path as a car barrels down the road. The car is travelling faster than usual because of the early hour and empty roads. The creature looks up in time to see its predator, and a split second later, between life and death, the skunk attacks the car with its only weapon— both inadequate for the situation and pathetic in its impotency. But this action does have an outcome. The creature heralds its own death and requires its life to be considered by some of those living in the immediate vicinity. At least for a moment, we experience the finality of the creature's life. Some of us will care just a little that she did not make the full journey, perhaps to where, after foraging for food, her young still wait.

To me, this small incident is convincing evidence of the unconscious brutality of man and his inventions in collision with nature. When I become aware of this creature's passing, I am drawn again to one simple truth about life—the understanding of how quickly it can be taken away.

HOSPITALS AND ALL THAT JAZZ

Just watched an old movie called *Hospital*, written by Paddy Chayefsky. It is about a large and dysfunctional metropolitan hospital in a past era, one I am familiar with. The story was not so important to me, but the ambience was. It allowed me to reflect upon the last few years, when I spent so much time in hospitals with you.

It reminded me of the RI Cancer Center (which was *not* dysfunctional) where we found ourselves every two weeks, and how each time we had an appointment, the drill was the same: pay, register, then put on an identification bracelet. The staff was diligent about confirming the information on the bracelet, even though they already knew you by name. I recall their cheerful attitude, greeting you as if you were there to be treated for a common cold, and I can still see all the patients in various stages of disability, sitting around the waiting area. I wondered how the staff managed to get up each morning, when the patients they greeted so cheerfully and treated so attentively would soon no longer be alive. A moveable sea of dead people walking. I remember everything about that place, knowing it would be here long after we were gone. The view from the window looked onto a paved pathway made up of commemorative stones, which led to a patio where hospital staff would gather. I used to flip through the worn assortment of magazines that never seemed to change. I noticed that an effort was made to make the environment decorative. Cut glass panels were added to the partitions that separated the infusion rooms from the main hallway. I would wander up and down the hallway, passing by the other small infusion rooms, where I could see people, some alone, others with family or a friend, all participating in the various rituals that take people's minds off the reason for being there. I wondered how long each of them would have to endure their treatment and how many would survive.

When I was not pacing the hallways, I sat with you for the duration of your treatment. I always remembered to bring the book you were reading, so those long hours would go by more quickly. I gained an objectivity regarding these surroundings. I took myself out of the peril of the moment, and found a way to make being here the activity of the day. As you grew weaker, getting you in and out of the car and into the building became more challenging. I found myself going about the routine of this new life as if it might go on forever. This was simply the new paradigm, the life style we had fallen into.

I was at the hospital today, this time to keep an appointment I had put off for over a year because I wasn't able to leave you. Many months have passed since our weekly visits to this hospital. You have been gone that long. What struck me as I began counting up the months was that only a decade had passed since my own bout with disease, and my frequent visits to this very same building. Yet, it seems like yesterday. You were healthy then and I was not. I was very ill and transformed by the medications. You looked after me and supported my fragile existence. I was grateful that you were with me and watched over me and took care of the things I could not. I guess I finally returned the favor. After my appointment, I walked through to the cancer center and up to the second floor's infusion area. It was the first time I was back here since the day we were informed that they could do nothing more for you. As I suspected, nothing had changed. The waiting room was full—women wearing scarves to cover their baldness, men with canes, hooked up to oxygen tanks. I turned away almost immediately, ran down the stairs, and walked briskly, head down, to where my car was parked. I no longer have an orange card, given to show that my car contains a cancer victim, permitting us to have a valet parking attendant, or use a designated free parking space. The need for that has passed. How often I thought that privilege was given us because it was the least and quite probably the most they could do.

THEY SAY IT TAKES A YEAR

Human beings seem to like to quantify things. Prescribe, analyze, and generalize. So it is said that it takes a year to stop grieving for parents, two years for spouses, and probably a lifetime for a lost child. We quantify our grief in time spent. I am closing in on the one year anniversary of your death, but I knew what the outcome of your illness would be long before then. We are all made differently and there is no time limit for grief, only a shifting of its power in our daily life. The fabric of grief is layered with many weights and textures and the colors seem to change with each day spent. Has one day gone by without my thinking of you? I wonder if I will have enough days left in life to know a day in which something of you is not tangible. Perhaps the follies one goes through in the process of trying to recreate a life will eventually amount to more than just foolishness. Maybe an extraordinary moment will happen, and I will understand the reason for being, and feel content that I am alive. Perhaps I will remember my life with happiness, and recognize that it was good. This may allow me to greet death with the same elegance you did. It seems a sacred endeavor. Each of us, one by one, will, at the appointed time, step off the train. When I am feeling optimistic, closer to the source, I sense I may discover what this time on earth was for.

I am at the Boston Airport, starting a trip that will take me to Germany and later to France, I find myself ordering a beer. It is what you would have done. It is not my drink of choice. The first taste is like a salute to you. Now as this journey begins, a widow traveler, I am wondering how I'll manage, and what it will feel like. There is no good way of knowing this in advance. I will take my temperature along the way. The first opportunity is right here, as I stop for lunch. Ordering that beer emphasizes to me how much I still need to relive older memories. The first taste is like a sense memory allowing me to recall how long it has been since I have had a glass of beer and, indeed, how long since you were able to enjoy one. For the last years of your life you were denied your simple pleasures and after a while even they didn't matter. So with the first sip, I feel a rush so distinct that it is as if I have called up and received the essence of you. I feel closer to you than I have been able to feel in some time.

In the airport café, I am seated next to a professional woman who clearly lives in them. I listen briefly as she chatters on her cell phone, portfolio open, being busy. In this environment, I am so entirely aware that you are not here. And yet I can see you stuffing your worn wallet into your back pocket. The space you occupied in so many of our trips is now confined to the past. Someone asks if the chair next to mine is taken. I say, "No, not anymore." It's a new world for me and I feel apprehensive about what I will experience when I land in Paris, where I will need to catch the plane to Frankfurt. You are present as clearly as the crystal heart I am bringing to your nephew, its cut facets sharpening my memory with images of you that go back for twenty years.

I had to come back to the place where you were born and where we'd spent quite a lot of time. I felt that if I were to visit once again, cradled in the familiarity of what had been, perhaps I might find a way to reconcile your absence. As the plane approached France, I chose to listen to a Beethoven violin concerto. The music came in strong through the headphones planted in my ears and once again I realized the power of music, particularly when it is connected so directly to my body. All other sounds and stirrings are gone and only the music has life. The plane might have gone down for all I knew or cared. You felt close to me. I hoped that perhaps this would be the last sound I ever heard. Of course I wasn't allowed to stay either serene or tragic, as the mood that enveloped me faded when the plane touched down.

It is now late at night. I have arrived at the DeGaulle Airport, my first stop. Now I find myself having to negotiate the next leg of my journey, the tedious, tiring and thoroughly disagreeable experience of traipsing through the miles of corridors and crowds to show a passport, to find the next terminal, to be frisked while my possessions are searched and to finally reach my destination. Now I am in physical pain and completely exhausted. I wonder at this moment if I should even have come. Could anything like closure really happen, or am I in for the disappointment of reaching for something that is not there to grasp? I make my way through a labyrinth of halls and passages, lugging my baggage. The bags, which I thought were light, grow heavier with each step. I move from one terminal to the next, miles apart, and finally, hot and tired, find my seat on the plane to Frankfurt. When I arrive at the Frankfort Airport, after a short, uneventful flight, I find no one to greet me. Ah well. I am not worried. I will just buy a ticket back home. This is my new way of coping with things. But then I gather my wits and finally see your sister who has been here all along. I am relieved to see her. We embrace, glad to be together again. Difficulty in finding her car leads to additional miles of walking. This is hardly the time to talk about you. We will leave for Hamburg in the morning and I have barely found the ground beneath my feet.

HAMBURG

My first impression of your nephew's wife, sitting in her beautiful kitchen having breakfast, is she is the same and yet she is different. Her speech is clear but studied. Her smile is distant. She needs help walking. But she is walking and can sit up without support. She is able to feed herself, to speak, and to ask questions. She is miles from where she started. But then I actually see her walk. This is hard for her. She is brave and resilient and almost defiant in her stubborn desire to be again as she was—a television celebrity, beautiful, active, and charming. And she is still beautiful in her new incarnation. It was important for me to see her and your nephew, as much for me, as for you. Their tragedy came just as our own was in its final months. The news of her brain trauma was shocking, dramatic and terrible. But it is still the story of love and commitment. When we were told about it, we could hardly believe it and, often in tears, we followed the progress of her fight for life. It is a parable: a beautiful successful couple with their world intact, all the ingredients in place—money, fame, a strong love and a balanced center. Sickness comes along and all that they have achieved hangs in the balance. It is a story of struggle, still unfolding, though it is remarkable that from total darkness, they have emerged to the point where they are now. And it is still difficult. How they manage from now on is still

129

uncertain. Faith and love will either heal them, or the moment may come when they will suffer some more. It's a chancy business and devastating when one realizes that such trauma is possible for all of us, and there may be no road back to the comfortable place we always assumed we should be allowed.

You would be a bit sad to see her now. You admired her beauty and grace. Your love and appreciation for beauty in general would make it difficult to accept the cards that were dealt them. But you will sense how remarkable she is in the way she has persisted and come this far, and the way your nephew has devoted himself to her with patience and real strength. You will have to acknowledge how courageous and noble these two people have been. And you will wish, though you are no longer here, to encourage and assure them that this adversity can be minimized, and that their lives will be long, meaningful and loving. That is what we all wish for them.

Later in the day, we are at a restaurant, not far from their house. The staff is very friendly and accommodating. The lunch is served beautifully but somehow I am not enjoying the tastes. She is wearing dark glasses and a hat and I don't believe anyone recognizes her. It is a pleasant lunch and I am quiet. I have yet to hear your name brought up, or any questions about what is always on my mind. My interior light bulb switches on. This is what happens to people. They lose husbands and wives. No big deal. It is natural. Except, of course, it's more complicated than that. Others do not recognize that there are some of us who are still twenty five years old in spirit and wish life to be eternal. For us, it is not natural. I do understand that what is happening in their lives is consuming and challenging, making it harder to think beyond their own real concerns. Yet the glue that binds is missing. You are missing. I feel I must be patient.

The next morning there is a long breakfast in their sunny dining room, splendid with flowers. I notice that about European homes. They are always filled with fresh flowers and candles. We tour Hamburg's points of interest, which serve to remind me of our tour together just a few years ago. My neck and back are painful, consequence of that long walk at DeGaulle, carrying that heavy carry-on. It will bother me till just a few days before I leave for home. I still wait for the conversation that will allow me to talk about you. But there is a polite silence and the subject does not come up. Except with your sister who is also here with me in Hamburg. We are able to talk together. She is welcoming and seems to understand the state of my loneliness and the loss that I feel, because she has experienced a loss too. While she has her own worries, she seems to be glad that I am here. I am concerned that I will be visiting for too long a time. Still, she seems happy to have me here and I am glad to be with her. She goes through photographs of your childhood, and reminisces about what she remembers of your lives growing up. I feel she is a friend.

A day later your favorite cousin arrives at your sister's home. He is full of energy and warmth and is the first one to speak as if you actually existed once. He brings with him gifts and a brochure showing the buildings he has designed. He brings something of himself to present to me. His wife sends along a small painting she has just done. He happily recounts stories of your shared childhood. He tells of your near drowning in the canal used by rowers when you were just ten years old and not yet a strong swimmer. He was fourteen and a better swimmer, but the current almost took you both away. He talks of the many hours the two of you spent whittling and making airplanes. He smiles as he recollects all those early moments. I listen to every word as if each is a diamond I want to hold.

When one has had a powerful experience there is a need to share it, to give it life again. You, Dieter, were that powerful experience and now you are no longer here and cannot share in the moments that gave so many of my experiences meaning. Most important, I cannot share the experience of your death with anyone. No one is really opening up to allow me that opportunity. I can't bring you back in any form, and know that is what I most want to do. I find myself instinctively turning to you, wanting to whisper what is on my mind. I want to laugh with you as we once did, look at each other knowingly, and in that look understand that we are in the same place. My instinct to do that is still there and I am surprised when I realize there is no one to turn to. Is it then all past? Is this just the waiting period between life already spent and the end game? Maybe it will not be a long time, or maybe it will be much too long.

NO MENTION - NO REMEMBERANCE

What was I hoping for? Perhaps that I could claim you through other people's memories. I was convinced you would be the topic of conversation from those who had such a close connection to you. I was sure if I associated with them, I would find you again, the way I did when I stroked the furniture you made in order to feel you breathing again. I wanted people to tell me that they missed you, how important you were to them. I wanted them to talk to me about you. To tell me stories I had never heard before, or even repeat the ones I had. I wanted them to understand the pain I was still in. I wanted them to know that I had been through something. That is what I wanted. But so far, there is a polite distance, a reasonable wish not to pain me. I know that. Yet it disap-

132

points. I want to tell everyone how impossible it is that you are dead and gone. I have come to know all these people, because of you. Now, I wonder why I am even here without you. I am learning that I am the only person in this relationship still standing. My circle was enlarged when I met you and now it has been diminished, which makes me confront the realization that I will have to reckon with: Can I really be your stand-in?

WILL THERE ALWAYS BE PARIS?

You would say Foolish Girl! Didn't you understand this is what would happen? (Or is that me, saying it for you?) I have never felt so unattached as I do these days in France. It is without joy that I find myself retracing so many of our steps in the city of lights. It had previously represented only joy. The magnificent buildings hold no magic. The energy of the busy streets and bistros seems routine and dull. The ambience is not welcoming. The underground is crowded and unpleasant. It is, I am sure, my own perceptions that are unpleasant and reflected in the surroundings. When we were here together, there was wonder in all we saw. We found ourselves in new and different adventures. Every day we were here together would forecast some excitement. My hope to hold onto what was ours is clearly not possible and I find myself longing for this trip to be over. I cannot say where my place is, but right now, it is not here. Perhaps it isn't anywhere. What is out of my control is how exaggerated the pain is, and how it is accompanying me everywhere. I foolishly thought the opposite would happen. I am in the midst of other people's lives and feeling displaced. I am not given the time or opening to talk about what is in my heart.

I needed a long and friendly path to open up for me to walk on slowly with our friends, to be able to speak with clarity about what I am thinking about all the time. Here it seems even less possible. No one seems capable of being candid or able to confront openly the reality of what did happen. Or they have confronted it and have moved on. I am being fit tightly into the life that others are living. There is no welcoming space. I find myself brooding even more. I can't make myself laugh or fully participate. I can't make others laugh either. My presence here is strangely awkward. I feel like heavy baggage. Old friends are trying to entertain me, probably exasperated that I am not enjoying it. What I want is their full attention for just a moment. The light turned on to what is my very personal heartbreak. But it doesn't come naturally and I realize that while that is what I want, I simply don't know how to ask for it.

What I need are friends who will be totally in it with me, without attempting to distract me. The pressure that builds up when people deliberately avoid speaking of your death is more intolerable than I could have imagined. It is unfair to try to reproduce you through those that cared for you. And I realize that is what I have been trying to do. That magical and unreasonable thing is all I want. Recognizing this failure in logic, I am counting the hours until I can be home, where life is not better but I can burrow into my own warren and find sanctuary. In what? I simply don't know. So I feel the pain of a broken connection. You will likely say, "Yvette, you are making too much of this." And I will say, "I am not so sure."

THOUGHTS OF HOME

In Europe, I notice the sky changes constantly. The sun goes in and out. The wind kicks up then dies. The rain falls then stops, and falls again. Sometimes I am happy to think about being home, the place that is most familiar, where the rhythms are my own. To be away from what is recognizable and commonplace is mildly disorienting, but I need this change to step outside the reality I have created for myself. Although I was born in Europe, I am only a visitor here. I often think that being transplanted from the place of my birth has separated me, in a profound way, from what should have been most recognizable. When I am here, I sense it would have been right for me to have been raised in a European city. When I am here, I feel I am home, but know that I am a stranger. There are marked differences here, and many of them feel comfortable to me. I am drawn to the surrounding history and antiquity as well as the style of modernity. I feel an intimacy that is unexplainable. It is a feeling of knowing that comes from a source bred in the bone. Beyond the open markets, the way coffee is served, the sense of authenticity, the aesthetics, and a certain civility, I am struck by a distant but familiar memory, unlived, but somehow known.

CUTE AND SILLY

Cute and silly were two descriptions of us that would seem to be inapt. When a woman is just three inches shy of six feet, with a naturally serious bent, it is hard to find the descriptor of cute remotely likely. And yet you found me cute in some of my gestures and imitations and general disposition. You brought out all the facets of the chameleon personality that I often hid. You were privy to that side of me that rarely surfaced, because there was so much freedom in our relationship that it loosened the definition of who we were. Standing at six feet four inches, you had a dour look most of the time and a view of the world that was always penetrating and composed. But this revealed only a part of who you were. Those who did not know you well might accuse you, and often did, of being arrogant. But you were capable of becoming absolutely silly when you found yourself free to express that side of yourself, often bemused as you entered into the world that we shared. With an almost surprised and defensive tone you would say, with kindness and gratitude, "You have allowed me to be silly." That playfulness is among my most treasured memories.

LETTER TO A FREIND - MAY 10

You ask about our relationship. Well, I might be accused of painting too rosy a picture of it, but the fact remains, it was amazing. One thing that simply did not exist was jealousy in any form. Any success either of us had was jointly experienced. He was proud of my life before he met me, a little in awe of its nonconformity, but those past years do not compare with the joy of a perfect relationship, living well, and feeling fully alive.

I will always know that a true gift was bestowed on me, some sort of divinity that allowed me to live blissfully for so many years. Why should I wish for more? Through all our life together, we hardly had a day in which we were not thankful to be together. All the trials and experiences that came along were like white water rapids that required navigation and a strong sense of the current, but we were always up to the task. There was hardly a day that he did not tell me in word or deed that I was loved. There was no one I would rather have talked to. We never stopped having long and discursive conversations. Mostly, we never tired of just being together. It was only eighteen years, but he made me happy every day. I hope to know that feeling again. I hope the memories will encourage me to someday go at this life by myself.

You may laugh a little when I tell you how I try to find solace in this new life. I begin to imagine all the things I will do when the mourning has finally lessened. I visualize life as it could be. I imagine myself as a vagabond, travelling the world without a destination. Perhaps, I think, I will work for an NGO somewhere in Africa or in the jungles of South America. I will be that enigmatic, anonymous woman who simply gives a helping hand, because she has no future to worry about. I may do this or I may do that. It is all totally and completely unrealistic— but possible. I am within myself so much these days that it is hard to imagine any of it will ever really happen. Even the news comes through to me heavily filtered by my own streaming thoughts. This is what solitude must be. Pretty word, solitude.

MANY OTHER DEATHS

I went to a memorial service today for a person we knew. When you died, I could only think of what I had lost. Since then there have been many other deaths: friends, acquaintances, their dogs, their parents, famous people we have come to regard as the voices of our time. The memories of those we have known, and what they meant to us, become more vivid. How temporary we all are! Life is a moveable feast. Nothing remains the same. Change is the fixed reality. That notion strikes me, in the latter part of my life, as an opportunity to continue to ride the big wave and glide back to shore. We must be present. Whether or not a circumstance overpowers us, we should have confidence that we will go back out and try again. If we can do this, I am convinced we are still truly alive. Perhaps the real high we can experience in life is to force ourselves to not give up. To make the effort and not be concerned with the result. Succeed or fail, we must try again. In our last moments, we should be able to look back and say we did our best more often than we did not.

MOOD SWINGS LIKE A PENDULUM DO

The evening seemed to come at last. Such a long day, and though the light was still strong, an overpowering fatigue washed over me, and I knew this day had come to an end. And with it, a time in which I felt strangely unglued. My mood has dropped to below ground level. Disquiet has encircled me and I want only to find my bed and make the day go away. The calendar explains my mood. It shows the days are inching one by one towards the anniversary of your death. So the reason is not hard to find. Yet it still surprises me. Yesterday I felt rather happy and strangely content. How quickly one slips from smooth stones to jagged rocks and loses one's footing. Life's terrain is treacherous, yet I feel as I fall, I am still able to dig my way out of the crevasse. Many sink holes are still there for me to fall into.

A TWENTIETH CENTURY MAN

There are many thoughts that intrude on my meditations. My new occupation is trying to mend the harm to my body. But with each yogic breath, I almost hear you say, "well done, keep it up!" You wanted me to be the best that I could be, although you were satisfied with who I was, encouraging me in whatever I tried. While you were disappointed that your life was cut short, I know you were only sorry to leave me, not sorry to leave the world. You were spared the burdens, preoccupations, and style of our current world. In that way you were a twentieth century man who would never feel at home in this current century when technology is redefining the rules. It would have felt like an intrusion. I think often that you got off the train just in time. And since your departure, we have had earthquakes and floods and volcanic eruptions and the worst oil spill ever to contaminate our waters. Perhaps you would say: "And you are surprised, because?" And I would agree, but still, they come one right after another, threatening in some real way what we have come to know as our way of life. I wonder if this is a real omen that needs to be considered. Transitions take time and are not often understood till we can analyze them in hindsight. And I wonder if we have that kind of time.

This winter and spring have been catastrophic in the breadth and depth of the collisions between nature and man. Even our state experienced floods that haven't been seen in a hundred years. That feels remarkable, but probably would not if I were a better student of earth's history. And the volcanic ash that kept planes from flying out of Europe for days and days and still floats up in the atmosphere suggests just how vulnerable we are. Nature is completely disinterested in our modern world. Two hundred thousand died in Haiti in an earthquake that flattened Port au Prince, a combination of earth's mighty movements and man's greed in building structures that could not withstand a relatively mild quake. And now fifty thousand barrels of oil are being spilled daily into the Gulf. Another way in which man's needs and greed sully nature. Man and nature continue to destroy each other, and you have no part in it anymore. I often think that I am glad you are freed from concern over these things or anything else.

And then I look around at the microcosm that was our little paradise and see that it is being cared for; there is still life here. My son and his friends are tending to all its requirements. Each time my son or I add something new to the building, or clear brush, or plant a bush, I stop and wonder if it will make you happy. I talk out loud to you, saying, "I wish you could see this. Can you? Are you pleased? Give me a sign." No sign is forthcoming, yet I know you must be pleased.

MIND/BODY

During your illness I would have a pain now and then. I would wake up, my body stiff and unyielding and have to walk it off. I tired easily when I tried to garden or work in the yard. Bending too often brought on quite a lot of pain. I attributed it to a lack of exercise and did not pay much attention to it. A few months after your death, I realized I was having real difficulty walking, that my hip ached all the time. I would stretch and try and strengthen my leg muscles, but the pain continued and I felt as though I had tightly strapped steel bands on my hip joints. I began to wonder if this were the bodily reaction to months and months of such an emotionally painful experience. Perhaps my mind had overpowered my body, my lameness a function of how I was feeling, the outward expression of an inward spiritual and mental condition. I began to meditate, receive deep muscle massages that broke up the adhesions that had formed. After a few months, I began to feel my body relaxing, allowing me to once again walk without pain. This was a powerful lesson about how connected the body and mind really are.

VIEWING THE PARALLEL MONTHS

I am counting down the days now, remembering each day as it was a year ago. At this time last year, your grasp on reality was slipping, along with your ability to walk without support. Our lives had become narrower in scope and I had no capacity to see a tomorrow. You were now under the care of Hospice and new people continued to come to watch over you. I was afraid you would fall and that your mind had slipped away, yet you were still here. It was not clear how my life would change, or that it had already changed. I believed that when change came, I would be aware of it and part of it. Today is May 12th. The weather a year ago on this day, was cold and rainy. I hadn't yet taken the storm windows down. The spring flowers were later in coming, though the magnolia tree had more blossoms. You were not able to care about the flowering trees outside our windows that you had taken such great plea-sure in. (This year the flowers came earlier and have been more abun-dant.) As I compare the two years side by side, I recall that another two weeks will go by before it is clear that you are dying, and then there will be just one more month of further decline before you finally disappear from my life. Months are not a lot of time to return to normal, whatever normal means. I sense that I have not or will not find that place of perfect comfort again. I probably have come to terms with the reality that you

142

are no longer with me and you had all the life that was allotted to you. You were on earth for seventy years, and eighteen of those years were shared with me—in the scheme of things not much time at all. It was not nearly enough.

This year, unlike last year, I am tending to the gardens, fully aware that you are not here to help me dig the holes for the new bushes I am planting, as you had always done in the past—your sole contribution to the task of gardening, though you took great pleasure in watching life take hold. You won't be here for any of it. And it still matters. In just a few weeks, all seasons will have passed, and then I will be repeating the cycle again and wondering if there will be a time when I will be able to close the gap you left when you died. I walk through my days as if I were outside myself. I secretly hope that you will witness these moments. I continue to hope, too, that how I conduct my life meets with your approval and that you will not be disappointed when I fail to hold up my end of the bargain; the bargain we spoke of—that I will gain the will to again participate in life in a full and robust way, instead of seeing myself disembodied, my heart detached, watching myself as I attempt to negotiate life in my new role as a widow, such a woeful word. The mirror reflects all the lines that have formed on my face, a certain down turn of the mouth, a face that once smiled often. I touch life now as softly as a feather moving along in the breeze, barely grazing what is there, rather than holding on with a firm grip.

THE DARKEST TIME

Without meaning to, I match each day with its counterpart a year ago. I am now re-entering the darkest time. As I count down the days till the anniversary of your death, I clearly recognize the descending nature of the slide down to the last valley. I wrote to friends about your decline. I monitored each day. And yet it was not till the actual moment of your death that I became fully aware of how real it was.

Time has placed challenges in the paths of our friends. I am struck by the nature of time, visiting it through a new and clearer lens. There is no letup to the challenges people face. Since I have been in the misty haze of my own grief, I have lost sight of the difficulties so many people are going through. It is all there and always has been, but I am only now seeing it, as I wake from the stillness that strangely protected me. I am in a new tangle of anxiety, more aware of the flotsam left in the path of what has happened. For my friends and acquaintances, it is past history. There is the assumption that we all move on, and anyway life continues to throw curves that require our immediate attention. While the storms rage in other people's lives, my storm lingers too, though it is now not so violent.

You are still so prominent a presence in my life and still surround me. I see you now as the man who was my husband, not the patient who was lost to me well before you took that final breath. What I often find myself reading is the note you wrote and placed in a sealed envelope, asking that I open it only after your death, which you hoped would be a long way off. It was a short letter, telling me to be strong, reminding me of the joy I had brought to your life, and instructing me not to wallow in grief and mourning. You asked me to be brave, but to lean on others. You said that you would love me always.

THE INNER VOICE OF REASON

Before I knew you, there were years when I felt no great need for a masculine presence in my life. Since living all those years with you, that need seems more urgent. I am not entirely sure it is really what I want, and the vague desire may merely be another way of learning how to walk again. I am treading on thin ice and feel unstable. The conversations I am having with myself are full of confusion and contradiction. "Maybe I am too old. Maybe I am not so good looking anymore." Then I hear myself confronting that argument: "You are not so old, and not bad looking at all." My inner voice continues to quibble. "You are no longer strong." I counter with, "Yes I am. I am mighty," and then, the voice whispers, "Maybe you are not." I beat my fist on the table and declare, "You are without boundaries," but then I say, "No, friend, you have restrictions." And so the conversation continues. I wonder if I can harvest the wisdom I spent years developing. The argument begins again and I hear myself saying somewhat peevishly: "Oh yes I can, just watch!"

I took a train today and was unlucky enough to find a seat in a car with a young child, perhaps four years old, who found screaming was by far his best method for communicating his pleasures and dissatisfactions. His life would have been in jeopardy had you been there. His mother, completely ineffectual, tried to quiet the lad with an occasional shushing sound. That gesture used up her parental skills. People began to lose patience, and simply took their belongings and moved to another car. At some point, the little tyke began to use the aisle as his personal running track, and as he passed my seat for the twelfth time in as many seconds, I grabbed him gently by the arm, looked into his gleeful eyes, and simply but firmly said that he had to stop screaming now! He looked at me indifferently and never stopped running. My murderous inclinations were subdued as I began to remember our conversations on the topic of children. How could I not think of you at this moment! The episode would have confirmed your belief that children should be seen but not heard, and not being seen would be fine too. I was never able to convince you that children are intrinsically good. You would concede a bit, but firmly hold that as long as they were not sitting next to you in a restaurant, or a railroad car, you would be able to live with the fact of them. After spending two hours with this kid, I would have lost the argument.

TRANSFERRING

It is the 8th day of July today, and there is no doubt that there has been a definitive change in the life force in this building. This building had served three functions. A home, a workshop and a showroom. It was like living over the family store. Our private home was also very public. Strangers often came inside to look around, as curious about the building as what was made here. We accepted this public image and invited people into our home and often into our lives. It is a different place now.

The big change is the quiet that has taken over. Your spirit still resides in the trees, and on the ground, on the steps leading to the front door, and yet there is something completely different. The smell of lacquer is gone, and the sawdust no longer filters up to the second floor, and while vestiges of the past still float about, our home is infused with a younger spirit.

My son and his friends mow the grass, clear the weeds, and chop down trees. New walking paths have been made, new garden areas are springing up, broken windows are being replaced, and the voices of young people can be heard as they gather in the backyard, resting for a moment to have a cool drink. The dogs pad about the house, barking at sounds filtering in from the road. I am confining myself to the small corners of the house, squirreling into what feels like my portion—where I feel most comfortable. I do not want to spread out. I no longer feel possessive about this place. I am happy to give it over and see new life injected into it. The spirit that dominated this space for so many years has changed, and I am not unhappy.

149

HOSTING AGAIN

The other night I finally gathered up enough energy to host a dinner for friends who lost their spouses last year around the same time that I lost you. I had been having a hard time drawing on the energy that once came so easily. In the past, preparing a meal for company had given me so much pleasure. The preparation itself, and having people around our table was among my most loved activities. Only as I set the table for this gathering did I find gurgling up within me that old sense of joy. A small door opened, and I have begun to look forward once again to hosting friends in this house that had always been filled with friendship.

Tears form as I listen to the melody and the lyrics of this well known song which only Edith Piaf could truly capture. It belongs to her. Others who sing it are simply borrowing it. I repeat the words, *no regrets, I regret nothing*, over and over again, hoping that I will believe it. I have been playing the song for hours. I can see Piaf belting out the words, her voice strong and clear, even in her weakness, carrying each word to the last row of the music hall, her feet planted firmly on the ground, so that she will not lift off as she sings. The melody surrounds me with memories that are in lockstep with my soul. The cadence is brisk. The beat is subtle. Her signature song impacts me deeply, precisely because I am aware of how terrible her life was. How can I compare it to mine? She numbed her relentless disappointments and isolation with alcohol and drugs. If she was able to sing this song with such clarity and honesty, a song whose words say that she did find love, and that love, though tangibly gone, is strong enough to carry her for the rest of her life—so it seems I can find no reason to regret either. I did have you, Dieter. Wishing for something else has finally come to an end, and the fire of renewal has begun to flicker with a cold blue flame. I feel as though life has returned and the flame begins to glow a bit brighter.

This will be my final letter to you, though my conversations with you will not end here. I will include you in at least three different thought messages a day and many more conversations. I will share a joke with you or a well written article. I will feel your outrage when you listen to the false prophets. I will know you are scolding me when I forget to close the kitchen drawer. I will remember how your arms encircled me after a long day apart, how you placed them around my shoulders when you acknowledged that I did something well, or when you noticed that I did not take myself too seriously. I will sense your confusion and frustration when I bring another electronic gadget into my life. You will be present at night in the memory of how we wrapped ourselves around each other like a prayer and I will still feel the soft touch of our skin mingling. You will remind me when I have forgotten to call a friend, left the dishes in the sink, or have not read the front page of the *New York Times*. I will hear you tell me to get over whatever I might be obsessing about, and encourage me when I begin to wonder if I am up to a challenge. I know you will approve when I look for happiness again. You will nod your head agreeing that life is difficult, but I must keep going. You will remind me to give my life meaning but you will also acknowledge that I, too, must occasionally feel reluctant. I will see you in all the places we have been together. I wonder if I will ever receive a message or a sign that you are still watching over me. Will we only share the secret once I have taken my final breath?

Today is the sixth day of September, a year and two months since your death. Someone new is in my bed. I feel compelled to spend some time on the banks of the stream where your ashes floated away. I wrap myself in a robe and wander down to this sacred place. I begin a conversation with you. I ask if you might approve of the way in which I have entered this new phase of my life. I want you to give me an affirming nod. Should I seek and explore the feelings that still exist within me? Do you know that you are still my guiding star? Throughout this past year, I have wanted you to present yourself to me again. I have hoped that a magical moment would occur to convince me you are still nearby. But there has been no sign at all. I stare down at the flowing stream, watching the water rush over the rocks and pebbles as it flows down towards open water.

I hear the familiar strains of a violin concerto hanging in the air. I follow the sound, thinking there must be a source, but the closer I walk towards it, the more it fades. It is your way of telling me you have been paying attention and reminding me you have been listening. I sense a mild warning. I believe that you are asking me to remember I am still precious to you, that I need to be cautious, but I must try nonetheless. I must make the most of every day. Calm and reflective, I walk back towards the house. I know I have just received my wish, though so many questions still remain unanswered. The mysteries continue, and I know now that so will life.

Emerging:

The birds are back, early morning song
Shoots of grass and bulbs—new life
The earth grows brighter—comes alive
All are signs of spring.
The shoreline's sand is moist
Winter washed away
The sun glimmers through the trees
The thick cover separates enough
So the sun finds a spot to root
And I, standing in that spot,
Feel no warmth, nothing new at all
No ebb nor flow.
Every way that nature does emerge
From the dormant quiet earth
Signals joy, joyous yes, but not for me
I am firmly holding death.

If I have not already died, or if I die today,
Remember please
I was a heart that did know joy
Once a smile that lighted you
My laughter did encircle you
My body warmed and comforted you
My life did cherish yours.

Sit close and please remember this
Whatever is the matter—will matter less
Whatever is true—will soon be false
Whatever is wrong--will soon not matter
Whatever stays the same—will change
Whatever seems to be—is only fiction
Sit close and make me understand
That if I grieve for you forever
You will die again and again.

Yvette Nachmias-Baeu

Appendix:
Words from friends

Peace at last for our friend and brother of over 40 years. Our hearts are pained and we are deeply saddened.

Your long, loving vigil is over, and Dieter is now gone. You brought him across this bridge with faithful attention and loving care. You too have earned this peace. Now your heart can feel fulfilled, for you have been strong and able and brave. I promise you, Yvette, you will never be without Dieter, for he is in a sacred part of your life. You will miss his physical presence at first, but this will pass into a larger aware-ness of our lasting bonds with those we truly love. With my own lasting love for you.

Oh, my. This entire sad chapter was handled so beautifully. My deep condolences. You face great challenges, but you deserve great confidence in yourself.

I cry with you. I'm sure that he was ready. You have held back your grief for so very long and it is good to be able to let go.

We are both so, so sorry to hear this! We send you the warmest of hugs to comfort you. I just read this message aloud to George and had difficulty finishing it--we both have such great memories of Dieter [and you] to carry in our hearts. George is chatting away-- reciting all the Dieter-isms he loved: "George, you do know that you have married the biggest flirt here!"...as Dieter referred to me...The image of Dieter in that black & white photo on the ship that brought him to America... How he got along so well with everyone in our family...How he always refilled our drinks even before we knew we needed it...His smile and his laugh...The mischief in his eyes--and more importantly, how he loved you and cared for you...We send you our love always.

I feel so grateful, that you gave me the opportunity to be there with you and Dieter during the period before his passing. Thank you for the true honor.

We are on the train coming home to Rhode Island and we are tearing up. We'll be thinking of him and you.

We are so glad we knew Dieter, even if only for a short while ... he was one of the great things about living in Rhode Island.

I'm so very sad. I look around my house, and see the beautiful things he made for me. He was a wonderful, wonderful man.

I never had the opportunity of meeting you and neither did I have much of a chance to renew my friendship with Dieter. You may have heard through our mutual friends that we all had some good times together back in the late 60's. These same friends have related the very close friendship that the four of you have enjoyed over so many years and I have felt envious at times. I am writing only to let you know that someone all the way over in Norway is thinking about you.

Bless you for all your love and goodness. Dieter is now at peace, as I pray that you are also. Beautiful note . I know that a deep peace and gratitude will fill your heart, for honoring his last wish, to die at home and only another woman who has done this same thing knows the cost-- but also the great value and gratitude that it brings--good job, sister!

Dieter was a noble man and you must be very, very proud of him for all he accomplished. He died with dignity. You are an example to everyone and his loss is felt by all of us.

You have been on my mind so much over the last weeks. Your love for Dieter, your grace and largeness of heart all shone brightly in all your notes –in your words, your outlook, your whole take on your situation. It's probably hard to see, and possibly irrelevant to you right

160

now, but I want to tell you that you have set an example of love and forbearance combined with your wonderful feet-on-the ground quality. For this I am deeply grateful. You gave so much by your example, when perhaps you thought you were giving little.

As I think back on what turned out to be a most fortuitous Saturday afternoon when we first came to the mill two years ago, we were to become the lucky ones to meet you two and to come to know our first new friends. We both value times we spent together and we honor the memory of a most special human being--brilliant, talented, engaging. Dieter will be very much missed by many but will always be remembered.

I knew him for such a short time and feel the loss. To you, the loneliness must be oh so painful. He was so bright, caustic, amusing, and welcoming. Though he is gone, your community of friends is here. Be kind to yourself.

We are so sorry for your profound loss, and hope that loving memories of Dieter can sustain you. We are also sorry that we did not really have the time to get to know him better. What we did know of him, over these past couple of years, we thoroughly enjoyed: his humor and intelligence, and his unique world outlook.

Our hearts go out to you in this difficult time. We have great memories of Dieter, of you & Dieter together, and of some very special moments which we spent together. Halloween at the farm. The Christmas Gala at your home. Dinner at the big table under the tiffany lamp--to mention just a few. He was and remains a bright star! He was truly one of the most interesting and well versed of human souls and we are sad that he is no longer sitting in the club chair in your home with a glass of wine and wit. We will raise a glass on August 24th and light a candle in celebration of a good man, and to the love you shared.

Please know that you have many people, some whom have never met you --that value you and how you have reached out to them. They are no doubt reaching out to you now, as I am. Keep your heart open to our caring thoughts and wishes for you, for they are intended to surround you with love and support. Having gained the trust, loyalty and caring of these many individuals, you have a veritable chorus of caring angels singing to your heart. We may not be in tune, but we are earnest and we love you.

Having spent time with you both we saw the special relationship you shared. It's rare to find a Soul Mate in life. It was obvious you had that in each other. You could not have been more of a presence. Dieter was very special to David and me as he was a genuine person, very bright and sincere, the kind of man who could stand alone with his beliefs and we will miss him.

Still absorbing your beautiful note about Dieter. How can someone you've known for such a short time make such an impact?

He was a genuinely kind person, whom I am proud to have known. I also feel blessed to have furniture that he made--and will remember him for his talent, his intelligence and his goodness. I'm sorry for your loss--and for the loss to all of us who knew him.

We have in our hearts that lovely week-end of the paintings, the only real time we had to get to know the lovely, intelligent person who was such a joy to your life. We have his beautiful benches and are reminded of his craft every day.

You have been a blessing to this group and to so many. I don't have the words to convey how much you mean to us, and the sorrow we feel for you. Know that you are not alone and that we deeply care for you.

I wish I had the words to console you, and to show you once again how much your presence in the group has meant to me, and to all of the people who have come to know you in this way. Dieter has been taken from you, and for that there is no consolation.

No words suffice. A great friend and master builder has passed. I will write again. Just to say now my spirit is with you in this impossible moment that is.

Yvette Nachmias-Baeu has led an eclectic life, following her wide range of interests to where they led. She has, for example, been a psychiatric nurse, a working actress, an advertising producer at a major New York agency, a farmer in Rhode Island, and a creative entrepreneur. A founder of the South County Montessori School, she also simultaneously opened a small craft shop which expanded into a highly successful retail business that continued for 12 years. At the time she met her husband, she was administering a Masters of Arts in Teaching program at Brown University and, while still holding the job, helped him to expand his furniture-making business to include importing French country furniture from abroad-- a business that allowed for a lot of memorable travel. In 1999, she contracted a rare auto-immune disease and, surviving it, volunteered as a health coach advisor for the International Pemphigus and Pemphigoid Foundation. Then, too, all the while, she's been writing essays and poems and is about to embark on fiction.

CPSIA information can be obtained at www.ICGtesting.com
Printed in the USA
BVOW041916271111

276851BV00001B/13/P